NOTTINGHAM IN 50 BUILDINGS

PROFESSOR IAN D. ROTHERHAM

AMBERLEY

First published 2025

Amberley Publishing, The Hill, Stroud
Gloucestershire GL5 4EP

www.amberley-books.com

British Library Cataloguing in Publication Data.
A catalogue record for this book is available from the British Library.

ISBN 978 1 4456 8688 2 (print)
ISBN 978 1 4456 8689 9 (ebook)

Typesetting by SJmagic DESIGN SERVICES, India.
Printed in Great Britain.

Appointed GPSR EU Representative:
Easy Access System Europe Oü, 16879218
Address: Mustamäe tee 50, 10621, Tallinn, Estonia
Contact Details: gpsr.requests@easproject.com, +358 40 500 3575

Contents

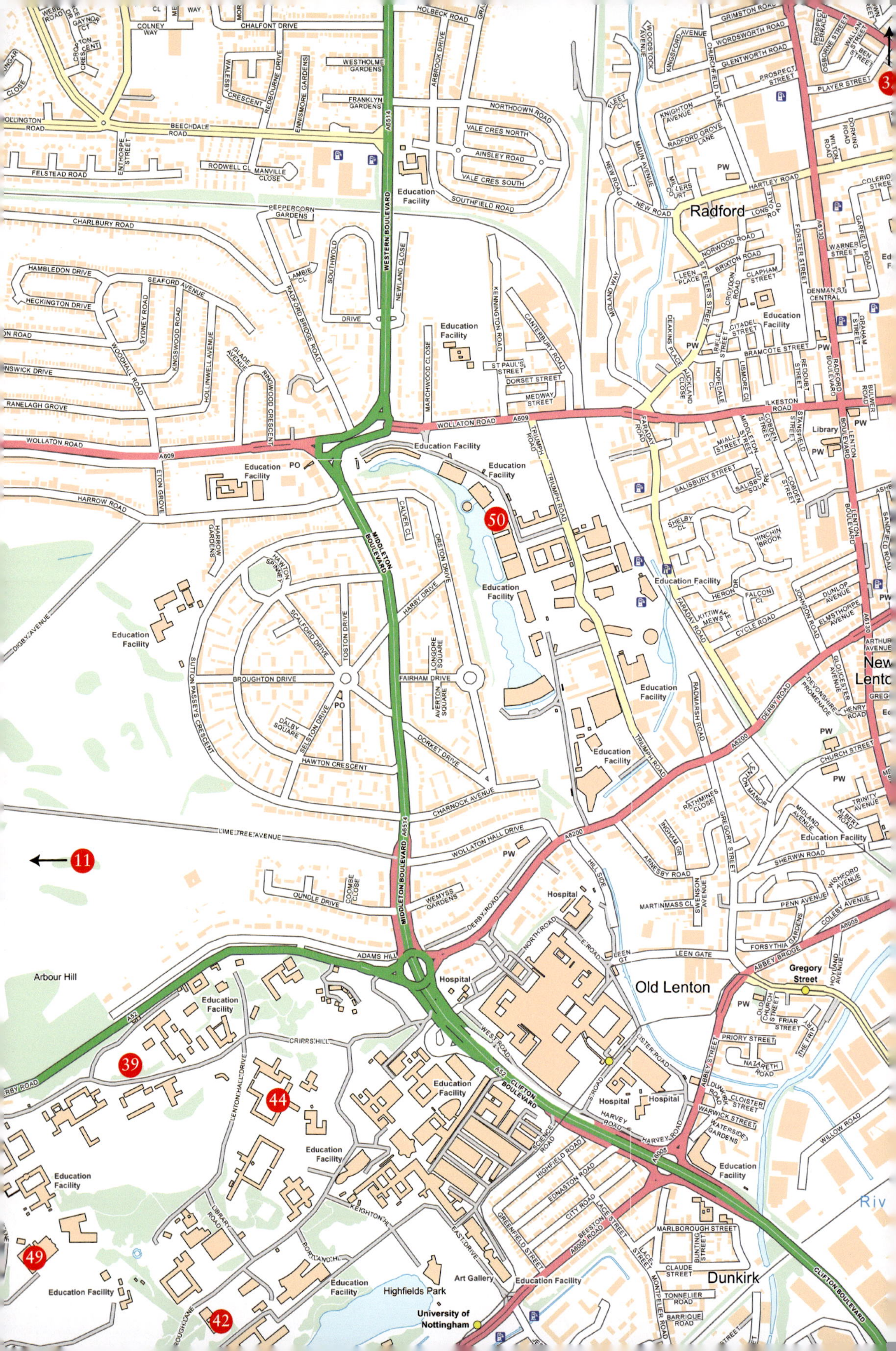

Radford
New Lenton
Old Lenton
Dunkirk
Arbour Hill
Highfields Park
University of Nottingham
Gregory Street
Art Gallery
Hospital
Education Facility
Library
PW
PO
50
11
39
44
49
42
3
WESTERN BOULEVARD
MIDDLETON BOULEVARD
CLIFTON BOULEVARD
A6514
A52
A609
A6200
A6005
A610
WOLLATON ROAD
DERBY ROAD
ILKESTON ROAD
BEECHDALE ROAD
CHARLBURY ROAD
HARROW ROAD
DIGBY AVENUE
SUTTON PASSEYS CRESCENT
BROUGHTON DRIVE
LIMETREE AVENUE
ADAMS HILL
CRIPPS HILL
LENTON HALL DRIVE
KEIGHTON HILL
PORTLAND HILL
LIBRARY ROAD
EAST DRIVE
BEESTON ROAD
LACE STREET
CITY ROAD
EDNASTON ROAD
HIGHFIELD ROAD
GREENFIELD STREET
SCIENCE ROAD
WEST ROAD
NORTH ROAD
HILL SIDE
LEEN GATE
ABBEY BRIDGE
ABBEY STREET
PRIORY STREET
NAZARETH ROAD
FRIAR STREET
WARWICK STREET
CLOISTER STREET
WATERSIDE GARDENS
WILLOW ROAD
HARVEY ROAD
MARLBOROUGH STREET
CLAUDE STREET
TONNELIER ROAD
BARRIQUE ROAD
MONTPELIER ROAD
BUNTING STREET
FARADAY ROAD
TRIUMPH ROAD
RADMARSH ROAD
GREGORY STREET
CHURCH STREET
TRINITY AVENUE
SHERWIN ROAD
PENN AVENUE
COLEBY AVENUE
HOLBECK ROAD
NORTHDOWN ROAD
VALE CRES NORTH
AINSLEY ROAD
VALE CRES SOUTH
SOUTHFIELD ROAD
NEW ROAD
HARTLEY ROAD
PROSPECT STREET
PLAYER STREET
RADFORD BOULEVARD
LENTON BOULEVARD
DUNLOP AVENUE
CYCLE ROAD
SALISBURY STREET
CANTERBURY ROAD
KENNINGTON ROAD
CHARNOCK AVENUE
WOLLATON HALL DRIVE
HAWTON CRESCENT
FAIRHAM DRIVE
ORSTON DRIVE
DORKET DRIVE
OUNDLE DRIVE

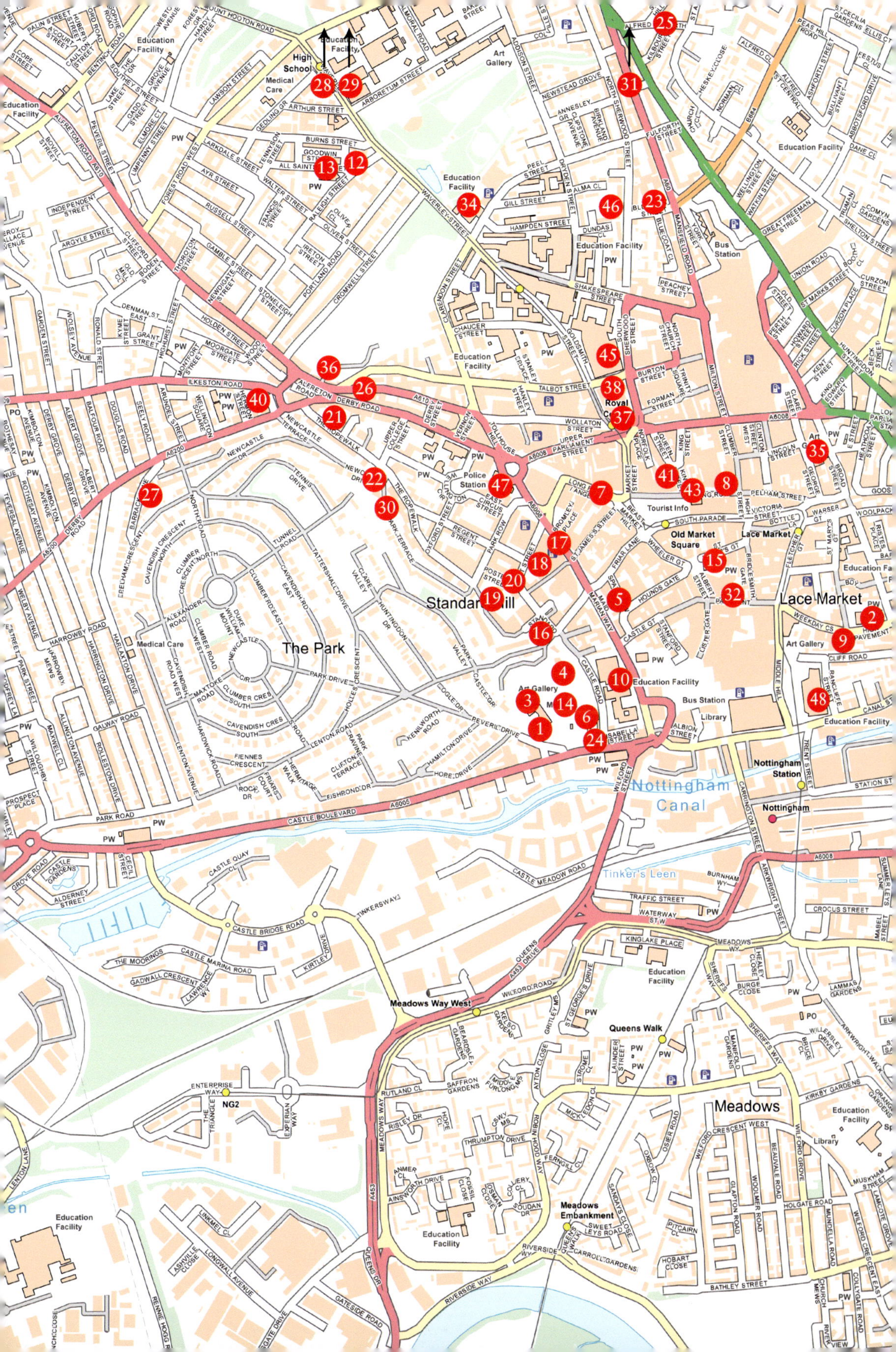

The Park
Standard Hill
Lace Market
Meadows
Nottingham Canal
Tinker's Leen
Old Market Square
Tourist Info
Nottingham Station
Nottingham
Royal Centre
Police Station
Bus Station
Library
Art Gallery
Education Facility
Medical Care
High School
Meadows Way West
Queens Walk
Meadows Embankment
NG2
ALFRETON ROAD
DERBY ROAD
ILKESTON ROAD
CASTLE BOULEVARD
MANSFIELD ROAD
WAVERLEY STREET
MEADOWS WAY
QUEENS DRIVE
WILFORD STREET
CARRINGTON STREET
ARKWRIGHT STREET
LONDON ROAD
CASTLE ROAD
MAID MARIAN WAY
CASTLE MARINA ROAD
CASTLE BRIDGE ROAD
RIVERSIDE WAY
1
2
3
4
5
6
7
8
9
10
12
13
14
15
16
17
18
19
20
21
22
23
24
25
26
27
28
29
30
31
32
34
35
36
37
38
40
41
43
45
46
47
48

Key

1. The Caves, off Castle Boulevard and Elsewhere
2. St Mary's Church, High Pavement
3. Nottingham Castle, off Castle Road
4. Nottingham Castle Gatehouse, off Castle Road
5. Ye Olde Salutation, Hounds Gate
6. Ye Olde Trip to Jerusalem, Brewhouse Yard, off Castle Road
7. Bell Inn, Angel Row
8. Ye Flying Horse Inn, Cheapside
9. Shire Hall and the Galleries of Justice, High Pavement
10. Severns/Severn House, Castle Road and Castle Gate
11. Wollaton Hall, Wollaton Road
12. All Saints' Church, Raleigh Street
13. All Saints' Church Multipurpose Hall, Raleigh Street
14. Brewhouse Yard, Below the Castle Rock, Castle Boulevard
15. St Peter's Church, St Peter's Gate
16. King Charles House, King Charles Street
17. Sheriff House, No. 64 St James's Street
18. No. 72 St James's Street
19. Nottingham General Hospital, Postern Street
20. Rotunda, Park Row
21. Ropewalk Pumping Station, the Ropewalk
22. Park Tunnel, the Park
23. The Old Bluecoat School, Bluecoat Lane, off Mansfield Road
24. Castle Works, Castle Road
25. R. Chandler & Co., Alfred Street North
26. Nos 126–28 Derby Road
27. Nos 1 and 2 Barrack Lane, Derby Road
28. No. 2 Alberta Terrace, off Sherwood Rise
29. Norris Ladies Home (Almshouses), Berridge Road, Sherwood Rise
30. No. 20 Park Terrace, off the Ropewalk
31. HMP Nottingham, Gatehouse, Perry Road, Sherwood
32. No. 10 Low Pavement
33. The Star Brewery, Radford Road
34. Waverley Building, Nottingham Trent University, Waverley Street
35. Watson Fothergill's Office, Nos 15–17 George Street
36. Nottingham Cemetery, Canning Terrace off Talbot Street
37. Theatre Royal, Upper Parliament Street
38. Royal Concert Hall, South Sherwood Street
39. Lenton Hurst, off Beeston Lane
40. Alton's Cigar Factory, Nos 154–62 Derby Road
41. Queen's Chambers, King Street
42. The Trent Building, University of Nottingham, Jubilee Avenue
43. Council House, Long Row
44. Cripps Hall, University of Nottingham, Lenton Hall Drive
45. Newton Building, Nottingham Trent University, Burton Street
46. The Hole in the Wall, North Sherwood Street
47. Nottingham Playhouse, Park Row, off Maid Marion Way
48. Nottingham College, Canal Street
49. East Midlands Conference Centre, Loverose Way
50. Jubilee Campus, University of Nottingham, Triumph Road

Introduction

Nottingham's name is derived from the word 'Snottenga', meaning 'caves', and connected to the Anglian tribe the 'Snotingas' that settled here from Germany around AD 600. The Snotingas gave their name to the settlements of what is now Nottingham, and that were first recorded as 'Snotengaham' or 'Snodengaham', meaning 'the homestead of Snot's people'.

One of England's top ten cities, Nottingham is known worldwide because of its association with the famous Sherwood Forest, Robin Hood, and the Sheriff of Nottingham. In terms of the latter, the first was appointed in 1449, making it somewhat too late for the King John connection! This historic city has a story that extends back to Norman fortification, earlier Saxon settlements, and older habitations. In the 1700s, traveller and writer Daniel Defoe described Nottingham, a settlement of just under 10,000 people, as one of the most pleasant, beautiful towns in all England. By the late 1600s, salt glaze stoneware was being manufactured in Nottingham. In the following century, the hosiery industry grew rapidly and lacemaking began. Nottingham was also home to other major industries, with bicycles, Player's cigarettes, and pharmaceuticals being just a few examples. The modern city emerged from its medieval origins into the Victorian industrial hubbub and is now the vibrant county town of Nottinghamshire.

Throughout the 1800s, the hosiery industry expanded and the town's reputation for lace made it famous with a lacemaking machine introduced in 1809. New industries were emerging to confirm Nottingham's growing status, with John Player founding his cigarette- and tobacco-manufacturing company John Player & Sons in 1877. By 1887, Frank Bowden was making bicycles in Raleigh Street, naming his company after the road, and by 1910 Raleigh produced 50,000 bicycles annually. On the back of such success, the town achieved city status in 1897.

Nottingham boasts two major universities, world-class theatres, and concert venues, plus numerous churches and chapels, schools and colleges, hospitals and more. It hosts two big, professional football clubs, the Nottinghamshire Cricket Club at Trent Bridge, and other sporting activities. It is also noted for its excellent shopping facilities and abundant eateries and entertainments. Associated with

The iconic Robin Hood statue at Nottingham Castle.

all the above is a rich legacy of buildings from modest to extravagant, and from old to very modern. Together these buildings provide the tapestry onto which is etched the story of this great city. The city today is changing rapidly, evolving to meet the new and emerging demands of the twenty-first century.

To tell this story in a selection of fifty buildings is a challenge, and this book addresses the task by taking the reader through a selection of some of the oldest and most historic structures through to the very modern. You could easily write a story of Nottingham simply through its splendid heritage of ancient public houses and their particular histories. However, this is a carefully picked choice from a variety of activities and functions to celebrate the evolution of the city of Nottingham. Indeed, it is immediately obvious when starting the task of compilation that there is an inherent problem, which is a surfeit of wonderful buildings and a remarkably rich legacy. Above all, Nottingham has a particular depth of heritage in its built past and these shops, business offices, houses, halls, pubs, and corporate buildings tell a unique story of a remarkable city. The sheer richness of the heritage resource is the key difficulty in selecting a mere fifty buildings. What to include and which ones to leave out becomes problematic. In making the selection there are some iconic structures which simply must be included, but I have tried to not just address the obvious ones that are generally covered. So, the selection includes more ordinary, day-to-day buildings that help tell the story of a great city and its residents through the centuries. Some of these structures can be discovered simply walking the streets of Nottingham and turning a corner to 'find' or 'discover' some hidden treasure that is part of the long history and fabric of the town then the city. With the commonplace houses, for example, there may be little in the way of recorded history of who designed and built them, though there may be information on residents in a particular area. With the notable iconic buildings there is usually detail of dates, architects, and those who commissioned them.

Placing the selection chronologically is also problematic since in many cases, buildings are multi-phased following initial construction. Bits are removed, wings and extensions are added, and significant parts of building structures are often replaced and, stone in particular, reused. This means that attributing a building to a particular time and phase of its lifespan can be very subjective and often not a precise science. In most cases, the selected structures are dated as at the approximate time of their initial construction, if known.

Finally, if you walk the urban landscape of Nottingham today, you discover on your perambulations the stories of England. This is a notable township from the Saxon era onwards and is geographically and politically a significant place with royal connections and architecture to match. At the same time, it is a place that has evolved from the hustle and bustle of the medieval market town into the filth and squalor of a Victorian industrial centre. It is also absolutely clear that there is – and perhaps always has been – a separation between the rich and affluent and the poor and downtrodden, and this too is reflected in the city's places, spaces, and buildings. Furthermore, evolving into a twenty-first-century centre involves almost constant reinvention, reuse, evolution, removal, and redevelopment, so this is not merely a grand conservation area but a working township. This brings me to a tension between a celebration of remarkable history, heritage, and people, and a mourning of loss and for missed opportunities.

Simon Jenkins (2003) forcibly made the point about the catastrophic losses of street heritage suffered by Nottingham. Whilst Nottingham was not alone in the twentieth-century destruction of fine, important, and sometimes commonplace dwellings of significance, it probably had more remaining in the post-1940s period than did other big cities. Today the city is once again restructuring its city centre core. Jenkins captured the sentiment this evokes with: 'Words fail me about Nottingham. In the years since the Second World War, this once-handsome hillside city has been variously punched, kicked and abused by its citizens. The new Nottingham is like a flayed skeleton to which patches of raw flesh cling bodily in desperation.' This is perhaps a little unfair; indeed, Nottingham is by no means alone in so freely destroying its heritage. We can only hope that lessons have been learnt for the future. However, in discovering Nottingham's less frequently trodden streets you will find hidden gems but also dereliction, destruction, neglect, and sometimes the abandonment of forgotten purpose. I suspect that, overall,

Nottingham has the richest resource of heritage buildings of any of the great northern or midlands cities and towns of England. But are these gems adequately appreciated and cared for? Buildings like No. 33 Castle Gate suggest not, and the view from Castle Road, for instance, highlights some problems of the twenty-first-century city. Perhaps the tour will help illuminate the answer.

Above: View from Castle Road.

Left: No. 33 Castle Gate, showing problems of dereliction and decline.

The 50 Buildings

1. The Caves, off Castle Boulevard and Elsewhere

Nottingham boasts Britain's largest known network of urban caves and caverns, with 800 or more mostly hidden beneath the ancient streets. Below the castle and running along the south side of Nottingham Park are the remarkable old caves for which Nottingham is famous, including the notorious and historically significant Mortimer's Hole under Nottingham Castle. Indeed, to celebrate this you can visit the City of Caves attraction where the biggest and most accessible sites are open to tourists. This underground history of the city results from the geology of soft sandstone which outcrops to form a distinctive hilltop and crag immediately north of the canal and now separated from the River Trent, its tributaries, and its floodplain by urban development. Indeed, modern Nottingham in many ways owes its present form and location to the fortunate coincidence of geography, topography, and underlying geology that created this low, well-drained, sandstone knoll so close to the crossing point on the river. The soft nature of the friable sandstone rock allowed early settlers to cut rock shelters in the abandoned river cliff on the south-facing side of the hill. From prehistoric times to the medieval, this was a good place to make your home. Today you can revisit much of this amazing underground network, a subterranean wonder created in part by nature and in part by people. Other local towns such as nearby Mansfield have cave dwellings, but only a handful. Nottingham has them in abundance.

The caves may have names that evoke their past, and their supposed or actual historic uses. Sometimes these caves were described as papist holes (i.e., for hiding Catholic priests during times of persecution), as chapels, and hermit dwellings. One house built over the caves by John Leavers was called 'the Hermitage', and it is believed that the Hermitage Caves along Castle Boulevard were probably used as storerooms, and fish caught in the River Leen (a tributary of the Trent that formerly cut close under the cliffs) were cleaned here for consumption in the castle. There was a medieval tannery and small holes in the rocks were probably used as dovecotes, again to supply the residents with food. In this case

Above: Nottingham Castle caves below the battlements.

Left: Nottingham Castle caves and Rock Cottage.

the doves probably provided winter food for the castle's inhabitants living atop this magnificent natural monument. Later usage included the caves being used as air-raid shelters during the Second World War, then in some cases they were incorporated into the gardens of newly built houses. Sometimes local people used them as storerooms or even garden summerhouses. Unfortunately, whilst many caves survive, a lot were lost to nineteenth- and twentieth-century industrial development.

2. St Mary's Church, High Pavement

Nottingham has a remarkable heritage of churches and other religious establishments from ancient, to old, to relatively new. Grade I listed as a building of outstanding architectural or historic interest, St Mary's is one of Nottingham's five Grade I listed buildings. The Church of St Mary the Virgin is the oldest religious foundation in the city of Nottingham; indeed, it is largest church after the Roman Catholic cathedral, and the city's largest medieval building. St Mary's Church is situated at High Pavement, itself a richly historic area. This is a parish church constructed mostly in the fifteenth century, but with fragments remaining of a late fourteenth-century building. The structure is of ashlar with lead roofs and has been modified and added to over the centuries. Not only significant citywide, St Mary's is also the largest parish church in Nottinghamshire after the Church of St Mary Magdalene at Newark. Located on High Pavement at the core of Nottingham's historic Lace Market district, the church is also called St Mary's in the Lace Market, and is a member of the Major Churches Network, and part of the parish of All Saints', St Mary's and St Peter's, Nottingham.

Presumed to be a Saxon minster but with rebuilding in the twelfth and thirteenth centuries (perhaps after town fires in 1140 and 1171), this would have been a dominant feature of the pre-Norman township. Today it is described as one of the finest medieval buildings in the country. Fragments of the earlier buildings exist within the current fabric, and others, such as two window arches in a local building, Birkin's Warehouse, are now separated from the church. This twelfth-century Norman window is one of the oldest surviving architectural relics in

St Mary's Church to show the tower.

St Mary's Church ornamental doorway.

Nottingham, perhaps from the church itself or the associated rectory house which predated Plumptre House. The church was noted in Domesday (1086), taking its origins back to Saxon (i.e., pre-Conquest) times. Much of the present building dates from late in the reign of Edward III (*c.* 1377) to the time of Henry VII (1485–1509), with the Gothic perpendicular nave completed before 1475. Other works were finished during the late 1300s and 1400s, with the tower dating from the time of Henry VIII (1491–1547). Owned by Lenton Priory from 1108 to 1538, the monks took the church living as rector, nominating a vicar to undertake the daily duties. In 1513, Dame Agnes Mellers founded a school in the church, the Free School of the Town of Nottingham, which lives on today as Nottingham

High School. This is an ancient church with a long and rich history including incidents such as when, in 1649, the founder of the Religious Society of Friends (Quakers or Friends), George Fox, was imprisoned for interrupting the preacher at St Mary's.

3. Nottingham Castle, off Castle Road

Modern Nottingham has strong Anglo-Saxon beginnings, with a Saxon settlement built on the high ground overlooking low-lying flood land of the Trent. The fertile countryside of the Trent marshes would have been valued for grazing, and the river itself, significant as a boundary, provided navigation and transport, and also fish and fowl for the table. From its Saxon beginnings, today's city owes its origins to the Normans, the builders of the first castle up on the rocky escarpment. This was adjacent to the 'French Borough', with the nearby Saxon settlement becoming the 'English Borough'. The combined population after Domesday (AD 1086) was around 1,500 residents, which at the time was significant number of people. Eventually, the two boroughs became one, with the English partition being the centre of the town's administration. This was the situation in the troubled times after the 1066 Conquest, as King William I ('the Bastard') set about subjugating his newly acquired kingdom. During the next 500–600 years Nottingham's history was closely connected to its castle, its strategic position and significance, and ultimately to national politics and power struggles. This situation continued up to and including the English Civil War of the 1600s. A consequence of this situation was that in 1651, after the Civil War ended, Parliament ordered Nottingham Castle to be demolished. This was to prevent it ever again becoming a Royalist stronghold. We know a good deal about the castle and its layout from plans and documents, particularly by John Smythson in 1617. The original defensive structure connected to today's castle site was built in 1067 to 1068, though it is likely that the location had settlement and defences from well before this time. Various monarchs from King John to Henry II, Edward IV, and Richard III all added to and enhanced this most significant of strategic, defensive positions. A separate building (Richard's Tower) was also constructed and fragments remain behind Castle Grove, but most of the substantial medieval fortress was destroyed.

Then, in 1674, the Duke of Newcastle acquired the site at a time when the need for fortifications lessened whilst aspirations for comfort and the advertising of political status grew. The result was that the castle was displaced by a grand ducal mansion with magnificent views to the south. By this time, the Duke of Newcastle was fabulously wealthy, and he commissioned his new house to be built there between 1674 and 1679. Perhaps in part because of their wealthy neighbours; in the streets around the grand mansion (still called the castle), affluent citizens began building fashionable villas and lavish houses. By the nineteenth century, the

Above: Nottingham Castle perched high on the rock.

Below: Nottingham Castle grounds.

then duke also had a mansion in the Dukeries and a major property in London. Nevertheless, the dukes might have been well advised to keep some aspects of the one-time defensive 'castle' in Nottingham.

The early to mid-1800s was a time of hardship and unrest, with many ordinary people very poor and often on the brink of starvation. Depopulation of the countryside through enclosures and the introduction of technology to displace people, combined with high food prices and a surplus of labour following the end of the Napoleonic Wars, to trigger riot and insurrection. At this time, Newcastle was the lord lieutenant of Nottinghamshire, and this was the time of the Luddite protests and more. This position of authority meant he was charged with responsibility for maintaining law and order and suppressing working-class unrest. His situation was despite the duke's personal concern for, and interest in, the conditions of the working poor, and consequently he was considered something of a reactionary, old-fashioned conservative oppressor.

So, during a period of particularly bitter political upheaval in the 1830s, the then duke was especially unpopular. One result of this was that in 1831 the Nottingham mansion was ransacked and burnt by the mob. There were attempts on the duke's London property as well. At Nottingham Castle, subsequent restoration took place, and in 1878 the building reopened as a museum and art gallery. Then, in July of that year, the Prince and Princess of Wales attended the formal opening ceremony. For anyone new to the city but interested in Nottingham and its history, a visit to the castle is an essential experience. From its elevated location you get a good feel for the place and its landscape setting. Nottingham Castle remains one of the city's most iconic buildings. Its prominent location, its place in Nottingham's history, and the spectacular views combine with the myth of Robin Hood and the Sheriff of Nottingham to lend an aura of antiquity.

4. Nottingham Castle Gatehouse, off Castle Road

The massive bases of the Nottingham Castle gatehouse towers still give a feel of the original medieval fortress. Indeed, this remains pretty much intact and, along with parts of the perimeter walls and towers, is the most substantial survival of the older structures. Built in 1251, the specification was for a 'good stone gate' and with its twin towers, gated passageway, and guardhouse is a substantial reminder of past glories. There was a moat or ditch, now mostly infilled, and the gate was protected by a portcullis with oak gates opening inwards. After 1651, with much of the castle reduced to rubble, the gatehouse was turned into a lodge and essentially allowed to deteriorate further until the early 1900s. At this time, it became a ticket office to the museum and gallery. Parts of the curtain wall south of the gatehouse also survive adjacent to Castle Road, and a walk along this stretch gives a good impression of the extent of the original fortifications and of the magnificent position of the castle itself towering above the high cliffs.

Left: Nottingham Castle gatehouse.

Below: Nottingham Castle gatehouse, showing the inside view from the grounds.

Nottingham Castle gatehouse with the massive towers from outside the fortress.

5. Ye Olde Salutation, Hounds Gate

There has long been a healthy rivalry between the ancient pubs of Nottingham, namely Ye Olde Trip to Jerusalem ('the Trip'), the Bell Inn, and Ye Olde Salutation ('the Salutation' or 'the Sal'), each claiming descent from the 1100s or 1200s, but in all cases not easy to prove precisely. The Blue Bell Inn has sadly morphed more recently into a café called Route One: 'An historic Nottingham city centre pub has reopened as a "premium sports bar" after a two-month revamp. The Blue Bell has been laid to rest and in its place is Route One, with food, cocktails, and a TV at every angle as well as a contemporary new look.' This is possibly now closed.

But returning to the others, the Trip and the Salutation can certainly demonstrate origins in the twelfth century. Although the Trip may have connections to the Crusades, the Grade II listed Salutation is in fact believed to be the older of the two, with parts of the present structure dating from the mid-1200s. There was a thirteenth-century alehouse, known as the Archangel Gabriel Salutes the Virgin Mary, described here in 1240 and a dwelling with outhouses and land recorded in 1414. The most obvious old part of the structure is probably the wooden bay, which is sixteenth century, though dendrochronology of the larger timbers in the building gives a date of 1360 for when the trees were felled. The pub certainly has a long, rich history with associations to local ecclesiastical foundations. It was said that crusading knights stopped here for food and drink on their way to the Holy Land. In 1336, when King Edward III stayed at nearby Nottingham Castle, many members of his court were put up here at 'Ye House by ye Sign of Salutation'. The name is derived from the greeting by the Angel Gabriel to Mary, though during the Puritan Commonwealth the figures of Gabriel and Mary were erased from the pub sign, leaving just the shaking hands. In the English Civil War, leading Parliamentarians, including Oliver Cromwell, were alleged to have signed King Charles I's death warrant in the inn. Then, with objections to the religious implications of the name, the alehouse was renamed the Soldier and Citizen. But in 1660, following the Restoration, the inn acquired its present name together with a sign showing a pair of shaking hands. There was also a brothel in what is now the dining room and a sweet shop in the Cromwell Room. By the late 1600s, the alehouse had a bad reputation as being frequented by highwaymen, including (of course, as is so often the case) Dick Turpin and John Nevison. The latter made the famous 200-mile ride from Kent to York to provide an alibi for a robbery, a feat that earned him the name of

Above: Wall plaque inside Ye Olde Salutation Inn.

Left: Ye Olde Salutation Inn.

'Swift Nick'. Further legend has it that Turpin was nearly apprehended in the caves below the inn.

However, there is much more to this old, Grade II listed pub, including historical anecdotes. These stories include the landlord in 1820 accidentally poisoning himself and his household with oatmeal laced with arsenic. It was intended to kill rats but had mistakenly been consumed by the residents. Old pubs also compete for resident ghosts, and the Salutation's landlord once claimed the presence of eighty-nine resident apparitions. Though how these were counted, and how much alcohol was involved, are both interesting questions.

The restored Tudor timber-framed building now stands alone on Maid Marion Way. However, perhaps the most significant part of the history and heritage is effectively out of sight with three levels of large caves used as cellars, including a well and a former cockpit for baiting and gambling. At times these caves were used for brewing but they also provided sanctuary for Jews escaping persecution and during one period were home to a colony of lepers.

6. Ye Olde Trip to Jerusalem, Brewhouse Yard, off Castle Road

Dating from AD 1189 and Grade II listed, this hostelry claims to be the oldest pub not only in Nottingham but in the whole of England. Located at Brewhouse Yard, Ye Olde Trip to Jerusalem ('the Trip) is described as an 'ancient pub built into stone caves with a charming, wonky interior and resident ghosts, plus food'. Indeed, Nottingham has long been home to great beers and wonderful pubs, with a number, including the Trip, dating back many centuries. Sadly, some, such as the Gate Hangs Well on Castle Road at the corner of Brewhouse Yard, were demolished, in this case in 1909. An ancient rhyme celebrated the old pub: 'This gate hangs well and hinders none, refresh and pay, and travel on'. Demolished about the same time was the Postern Gate on what became the main route into the Broad Marsh Centre, and the name presumably derives from an ancient gateway in the old medieval town. These are all very regrettable losses to the mid-twentieth century 'urban improvement' schemes which took their toll in many English towns and cities. Perhaps Nottingham lost so much more because it had much more to lose. The Trip provides remarkable insight into this ancient and historic part of the city, and on a sunny weekend is now a thriving city-centre hostelry.

As is so often the case with these multi-phase buildings that have so much local folklore attached to them, the precise dating is ambiguous to say the least. There were at least thirteen premises here with rooms cut into the soft rockface which were demolished in 1909. The Trip indicates what these were like, with networks of long, narrow cellars and a remarkable chimneyed brewhouse cut into the rock.

Above and left: Ye Olde Trip to Jerusalem.

Close-up of the entrance to Ye Olde Trip to Jerusalem.

First noted in 1618, the pub's name is only known from 1799, and a painted date of 1189 was described by Harwood (2008) as 'spurious', i.e. forged or at least embellished. Nevertheless, this intriguing public house is assumed to be medieval, and its courtyards led to a cell cut in the rock, perhaps around 1760 and probably once the publican's dwellings.

7. Bell Inn, Angel Row

The city has a wonderful and perhaps unrivalled heritage of old pubs despite some notable ones having been lost. One of Nottingham's ancient public houses, the Bell Inn on Angel Row, has a moulded pediment containing a bell above a large sign saying 'Bell Inn'. It has a medieval roof at first-floor level and there are spectacular caves under the inn, which are also probably medieval and when investigated revealed evidence of nineteenth-century occupation. The front of the building was substantially rebuilt in 1820, although it is described as having a fragmentary timber frame with claimed associations to the Carmelite friary from around 1276. First formally recorded in 1638, the premises were noted in the will of Alderman Sherwin when he left his share to the 'three parishes' of Nottingham. A crown-post roof was dendro-dated to around 1437, and when excavated the 53-foot (16-metre) 'Monks' Well' behind the pub produced debris and rubbish from the early 1400s. It is assumed there was an associated small brewhouse. The windows to the ground-floor frontage of the building have stunning strained glass which from the street view is illuminated by the lighting from within.

Above: The ornamental frontage of the Bell Inn.

Below left: The Bell Inn in close-up.

Below right: The Bell Inn with the leaded light window illuminated from within.

8. Ye Flying Horse Inn, Cheapside

This lovely inn – again, no longer a hostelry – is included at this early point in our timeline because of the claimed date on the outside the of building ('Est in year 1483') and the possible inclusion of some genuinely old timbers. However, all is not as it seems, since this is mostly, if not all, a five-gabled deception. The two west gables are nineteenth century, with one rebuilt by W. F. & R. Booker as a smoking room in 1875, and the three eastern ones make up the original inn. The other eastern gable was a remodelling of an earlier building. The impression overall is of a sixteenth-century, Tudor building, but this was the designer's whim; the architect, D. G. Millet, undertook work for Trust Houses in 1936, influenced by the inspiration of his native Essex.

However, the building is on the site of the Plumptre family house, which was erected in the thirteenth century. In 1400, when John de Plumtre founded Plumptre Hospital, the oldest portion of the Flying Horse in the Poultry was part of the endowment. By the eighteenth century the property was called the Travellers Inn, and in 1791 it was the Flying Horse Inn. By 1799 the Flying Horse was owned by William Rowbotham and noted as being at the Hen Cross. In 1818, the occupier

Above: Ye Flying Horse Inn.

Right: A close-up of the signage for Ye Flying Horse Inn.

was now a Robert Mackley, with the rent in 1826 being £63 per annum. The building was in a poor state and hardly habitable, but following repairs was demanding a rent of £100 a year. In 1832, the occupier was Jane Clark. Then in 1935, the building was substantially restored as described earlier.

There may be some genuinely old timber in the eastern wall, but the present building is first recorded in the early eighteenth century, with an addition by William Stretton sometime around 1782 to 1788. The structure has glazing from the mid-1800s with the front supported by columns, and it was recorded that there was stabling to the rear. Although no longer a public house, at least this building has survived and found a new use.

More recent history includes when on Thursday 24 November 1977 Richard Branson, John Mortimer, Johnny Rotten and others celebrated the not guilty verdict for Virgin Records at Nottingham Magistrates' Court. This related to the promotional poster of the Sex Pistols' *Never Mind the Bollocks* album in the Virgin Records store, No. 7 King Street. The old inn continued as a public house until 1989. It was then converted into a shop and is now at the entrance to the 'Flying Horse Walk' shopping mall. The building is Grade II listed.

9. Shire Hall and the Galleries of Justice, High Pavement

The Shire Hall and the County Gaol were built close together at High Pavement, now a notable heritage area of Nottingham connected to the historic Lace Market. The former building was first noted around 1375 to 1376 and subsequently extended in the 1600s. However, the floor of the ancient structure collapsed in 1742, with rebuilding agreed in 1767 and commissioned in 1771. This new structure was to a design by London architect James Gandon. Additions in the nineteenth century were by Henry Moses Wood and James Nicholson. The National Justice Museum (formerly the Galleries of Justice Museum) is also known as the Shire Hall, and now an independent museum. The modern museum is housed in what was once the combined Victorian courtroom, gaol, and police station, and is therefore a richly historic site. This was a place where an individual might have been arrested, sentenced, and even executed within those same premises – all very efficient!

The courtrooms date back to the fourteenth century, and the gaol is documented from at least 1449 when it was noted in Nottingham's Great Charter. The facility was mostly rebuilt in 1618, then considerably extended in 1833. The County Justices bought County House with a new men's gaol being built adjacent to Shire Hall, and a women's prison following soon after. Along with the courtrooms, the building was also used as a police station from 1905 to 1985. The facility including the courts finally closed in 1986. At the visitor centre, the former cells can be viewed along with ancient dungeons cut into the sandstone rock to provide a genuine, if rather grim, view of our former judicial system.

Right: National Justice Museum.

Below: National Justice Museum with the old blue light.

10. Severns/Severn House, Castle Road and Castle Gate

This is perhaps one of the most peculiar architectural gems in modern Nottingham. Probably built around 1340, this Grade II listed timber-framed building was on Middle Pavement until 1969. It was then a restaurant but was removed to make way for the Broadmarsh Centre, itself now demolished. Severns was, however, rescued and reassembled by F. W. B. Charles; the three-bay hall with a ground-floor shop and workroom was the front of a merchant's shop. There was originally a rear service range extending over the caves that are still present at the Broadmarsh site. From 1879 to 1885 the building was the offices of the architects Samuel Dutton Walker and John Howitt. The present name derives from John and James Severn, who were wine merchants on Middle Pavement and relocated to the property in 1900. However, in May 1941 roof of the building's yard was badly damaged in the Blitz. At the end of the Second World War the then owners presented plans to alter the building, and about the same time it was threatened by a desire to widen Middle Pavement. With all this in mind, plus the imminent redevelopment of the Broadmarsh area, in 1968 the premises were bought by Nottingham City Council. Supervised by F. W. B. Charles, it was dismantled and then reassembled at the present location from 1970, where it became a lace museum and shop from 1980 to 2009. Readers will be aware of central government directives for local councils to sell off potentially surplus buildings and land where possible, and this policy was combined with punitive cuts to local authority finances. One consequence was that many local authorities had to embark on what were in effect 'fire sales' of assets. So, in 2012, Nottingham City Council offered the Severns building for sale and in 2013, along with a number of other buildings on Castle Gate formerly occupied by a costume museum, it was sold to a local developer. Nevertheless, by June 2022 the premises were yet again changing hands and were once more on the market for an asking price of £499,000.

As with such restorations, not everything from the 1960s move is absolutely accurate but from a superficial look it seems pretty good, and at least the fabric has been saved even if the context is lost. Many timber-framed buildings in medieval times were from timbers hand-picked in the woodland and cut and shaped on site, then transported to their location and erected there. With this in mind, assembly on a new site is not so totally out of context. This is a traditionally constructed timber-framed building with a crown-post or 'king-post' roof where the structure rests on a tie beam or collar beam to support a collar plate. The building has timbers dendro-dated to 1334.

Below left: Severn House, now on Castle Gate.

Below right: One of Nottingham's most famous timber-framed buildings: Severn House on Castle Gate.

Road sign by Severn House on Castle Gate.

11. Wollaton Hall, Wollaton Road

Overlooked by its castle on the hill, modern Nottingham, from Victorian parks and botanical gardens to libraries, museums, art galleries, and theatres, is richly endowed with green, open spaces and superb public buildings. Of these, the most magnificent is undoubtedly Wollaton Hall and park, which, designed by Robert Smythson who also created nearby Hardwick Hall and Longleat in Wiltshire, has been described as the architectural sensation of the Elizabethan age.

Wollaton Hall was built from 1580 to 1588 by the nephew of the Duke of Suffolk, Sir Francis Willoughby (1547–96). With its fine parkland and a herd of red deer, it is a dramatic connection to English history and one of the country's most significant Elizabethan houses. This is a tangible reminder of an historic past, even though urban development has swept around and engulfed the old park. Cambridge-educated, Willoughby was a man knowledgeable about architecture and had extravagant tastes. Owning land with coal, the estate funded the £8,000 cost of the hall, though Sir Francis experienced periods of significant debt, perhaps associated with the consequences of his increasingly poor mental health. Various masons and master masons worked on the project and many ideas were copied and imitated by other housebuilders over subsequent centuries. The location is magnificent with the hall sitting on top of a hill and overlooking the earlier hall in the nearby village. With periods of financial cashflow problems and on an estate rich in mineral coal, some of the workmen involved in the building project were paid in carts of coal.

A costly venture by Sir Francis, the house was rather neglected after his death, since the family preferred some of their more luxurious properties elsewhere in the Midlands. The situation was further complicated by a bad fire in 1642, with restoration delayed until 1687. At this time, the house was lived in by Francis and Thomas Willoughby (1st Baron Middleton) along with their sister Casandra, and it was she that documented the history of the house. Various other repairs and additions took place throughout the 1800s, though the owners still preferred to have their main residence at other locations. With the social issues following the First World War, and the economic problems for many landed estates, the property was sold to the City

Corporation in 1924 and became a public park and museum. From 2005 to 2007 there was a period of major restoration of the house which was restored by Purcell Miller Tritton. The former stables now house cafés, shops, and facilities.

Nottingham seems to embrace the idea of tree-lined avenues and wide, open roads, and Wollaton is a great example of this. With museums, galleries, and parks aplenty, the city is well placed to provide a good quality of life for its residents. The contemporary hall holds and displays significant collections of paintings and a natural history museum. The grounds include gardens with a Camelia House which

Above: The spectacular Wollaton Hall.

Left: Ornamentation on Wollaton Hall.

An example of the carved detail on Wollaton Hall.

is the oldest cast-iron building in Britain. Furthermore, over the years, Wollaton Park has hosted numerous events and celebrations ranging from Salvation Army parades, and other religious activities, to archery competitions, and dog handling shows. One especially unusual time was when the park housed German prisoners of war with their distinctive uniforms sporting a 'P' in large print on the back. Also in the 1940s, the park was a temporary home to the US 508th Parachute Regiment. Today, this is just one of the numerous rather special open spaces within the city.

12. All Saints' Church, Raleigh Street

Old churches are frequently at the heart of English villages, towns, and cities and All Saints' Church, an Anglican church in Nottingham, is a Grade II listed building. The church was formerly the Parish Church of All Saints', Nottingham, and then became one of the two churches of the parish of Nottingham, St Peter and All Saints when they merged in December 2002. It later became one of three parish churches in the parish of All Saints, St Mary, and St Peter. The building is a substantial example of Victorian church architecture, built in the Gothic Revival style and designed by T. C. Hines. The spire is 175 feet (53 m) high and even today is one of the tallest buildings in the city.

Built from 1863 to 1864, mostly of sandstone, it cost around £10,000 (about £1.25 million) and was paid for by local philanthropist William Windley JP. There was also a large parsonage and a church school, with the overall costs amounting to about £25,000. All Saints' Church was constructed in what at the time was a wealthy, new suburb and was consecrated in November 1864 with a packed congregation of about 1,200 (in a church designed for perhaps 800) with many clergy also in attendance. The location was formerly Sandfield, but the village was subsumed into Nottingham in part due to the 1830s post-cholera expansion. By the 1940s, the area had declined into post-war poverty, and by the 1980s it was designated as an 'Urban Priority Area'.

In the late twentieth century, as with many urban parishes, the congregation had fallen to maybe thirty or forty people. The old school building fell out of use by the 1920s and was turned into small workspaces, with, in the early 1980s, half the sizeable vicarage converted to residences for young, single people. The old school building has been refurbished for local community use and the church itself still holds Sunday morning services but has possibilities of other shared usage.

Old churches frequently have individual stories and peculiar tales, and in this case, it concerns bells and pigeons. Damage to the church spire had allowed pigeons to enter the bell tower and nest and roost there. A consequence was that by May 2019 the bells had to stop ringing because of health and safety worries. Due to the copious amounts of pigeon guano, the floor about the bells had rotted. However, stepping in to help resolve the crisis, the Nottingham University Society of Change

Below left: All Saints' Church and a view of the tower.

Below right: All Saints' Church seen through the trees.

All Saints' Church doorway from the churchyard.

Ringers, with the support of the church community, set up a project to restore the tower. A complete clean of the tower was required and this resulted in the removal of over two tons of bird excrement. The old, rotted floor was dismantled, and a new floor constructed as a load-bearing platform to facilitate any necessary future work. There was also a full renovation of the ringing chamber, and from February 2020 the bells rang out once more.

13. All Saints' Church Multipurpose Hall, Raleigh Street

All Saints' Church was built according to plans by the local Nottingham architects T. C. Hine and Robert Evans, funded by William Windley, a Nottingham silk merchant. The site of the church is on the medieval Sand Field, preserved as common land north-west of the town until the 1845 Nottingham Enclosure Act. Windley funded the 800-seat church in memory of his first wife, Margaret, who had died in 1860. There was an eleven-bedroomed vicarage (including five bedrooms for servants), a church school catering for girls, boys and infants, plus a three-bedroomed, semi-detached house for the schoolteacher. At this time, the church school charged fees but then with the introduction of free elementary education for all, the All Saints' school was closed in 1906. Nevertheless, the Sunday school still thrived with 725 children on the roll, which rose to 845 by 1912. At this time the church was thriving with thirty-seven baptisms and thirty-two confirmations in the year to September 1912. Attendances at the church peaked in the 1920s when you had to arrive early to get a seat at Evensong!

However, following the Second World War the area went into a severe economic decline and the congregation followed. In more recent years there has been major

All Saints' Church's multipurpose hall, Raleigh Street, and the old wall.

investment to develop the multiuse facility for a wider community, the church and the hall reinvented their purpose. Financial issues were still a problem and eventually, in the 1990s, the buildings were acquired by the Community Development Agency. They are now described as 'Church schools, now community centre and workspace units' and Grade II listed, and there is a very old section of wall masonry preserved by the entrance to the present-day hall.

14. Brewhouse Yard, Below the Castle Rock, Castle Boulevard

Situated immediately below the Castle Rock is a row of seventeenth-century terraced houses adjacent to Ye Olde Trip to Jerusalem public house. Although they belonged to the castle brewers, they were at some point used by clothiers (framework knitters) who needed water from the nearby River Leen at the foot of the castle cliff. Proximity to a supply of water was also vital for brewing, and in 1621, the King granted permission for a brewhouse to John Mitten and William Jackson from London.

By the late seventeenth century, Samuel Wildboare lived at Brewhouse Yard with his family. Originally from Northampton the Wildboare family belonged to an independent church and came to the areas drawn by its extra-parochial status. They were comfortably off making their living as fullers and dyers of cloth. The eldest son of the family, Tobias, was also a land surveyor and preacher. William Elliott and family moved into the Brewhouse Yard cottages around 1732, and his occupation whilst originally noted as a stocking trimmer and dyer, was changed in 1750 to a 'gentleman'. It is believed that he may have made his fortune by the invention of a secret recipe for black dye, used for men's stockings. Later residents, by the early nineteenth century, were less affluent and times were changing. At this time the Lee family resided here, renting from the wealthy Norton family who owned the land. Whilst the Lees were not paupers, they were certainly not so well off as the Elliotts or the Wildboares had been. Charles Lee and his wife Frances were both traditional framework knitters, but this was an occupation was becoming less profitable because of new technologies as the industrial revolution changed working practice. An additional problem was the arrival of cheaper imports from Europe with the ending of the long-running Napoleonic wars. In Nottingham, the phrase 'as poor as a stockinger' became a commonplace. What followed were the famous Luddite protests and frame-breaking riots.

By the twentieth century, knitting frames had finally gone and the great lace factories of Nottingham had evolved, themselves to decline by the end of that century. The latest occupants of Brewhouse Yard were then the Webster family with William Webster, ironworker, but the others were connected to the lace industry. Daughter Lucy was a finisher in the Lace Market where she undertook tasks preparing lace for sale when delivered to Nottingham centre from the lace factories further away. She was one of the last workers here and, living a long life she left a good account of those early years when she was interviewed at the age of eighty-nine years, in 1982. The residents at that time got their water supply either from wells, or by purchasing buckets of clean water from private water companies. One such business was the Castle Pumping Station next to Brewhouse Yard which operated until in 1880, Nottingham Corporation took control of the town's water with a newly constructed waterworks. This provided plentiful, clean water to Nottingham and surrounding settlements, and the role of the Brewhouse Yard cottages was as the home of Waterworks staff.

The buildings are of good quality red brick and though, like many of the buildings associated with the caves, they incorporate earlier structures, the exteriors date from around the 1680s. One cottage has timbers dendro-dated to 1640. The service areas at the back were cut into the soft sandstone, and residents during the Second World War recalled needing to cover their cooking pots to stop sand falling from the roof getting into the food. This was presumably during air raids when the caves were used as shelters. An archway marks where a horse and cart might once have passed through to service the various commercial activities taking place. A second row of cottages was demolished around 1875, and eventually the site was acquired by the City Council in 1975, with the buildings being converted into a museum for the social history collection of the Castle Museum.

Above: Brewhouse Yard and the ancient caves.

Left: Brewhouse Yard cottages.

15. St Peter's Church, St Peter's Gate

St Peter's is one of the three parishes based on the ancient town centre of Nottingham. In the Domesday Book there is just reference to St Mary's, which was the pre-Conquest foundation set in the old Saxon borough. It seems therefore that St Peter's and St Nicholas' churches were established after the Conquest but probably prior to the twelfth century. This was in the newly established 'French borough' that grew quickly developed between the old Saxon settlement and the imposed Norman castle. The earliest reference to these two new churches was around 1108, as a gift from William Peveril to the newly founded Lenton Priory. The first church was constructed on rocks above marshland around the Rowell Brook. The area is now St Peter's Square, though for centuries the marshy conditions were a problem for the parish authorities. The early church would have been a simple building with a nave and a round apse, though we have little evidence since it was destroyed, possibly twice, in the mid-1100s. The church was then rebuilt between 1180 and 1220, and a south aisle added, and some of this structure remains today, possibly with some parts of the earlier structure also incorporated. In 1348, bubonic plague or the Black Death arrived in Nottingham shortly after the tower and spire had been added to the building. The impacts of the plague stopped any more construction work for some years afterwards.

Additional work was undertaken around 1480, with timber granted by Nicholas de Strelley taken from his estate outside Nottingham. However, construction at this time was not a precise science and the additional weight of the new stonework forced the ancient south arcade out of its true alignment. Whilst collapse was stopped by building new buttresses to the south aisle, the columns at the nave's east end remain visibly leaning but stable.

St Peter's continued to have a significant role in the church and in Nottingham society over the centuries and lengthy accounts of the church's history testify to this. There are some landmark changes over the period such as the 1500s separation from Lenton Priory because of the Reformation. In 1544, a washerwoman called Margery Doubleday willed a new bell to St Peter's and this was to be rung at 4 a.m. every weekday in order to wake her fellow washerwomen as one of the public roles of the church. However, there were signs of decline in the church's fortunes, and in 1559 Queen Elizabeth's commissioners reported that the curate did not use the English prayers required by the Act of Uniformity. Furthermore, the church was in a state of neglect and without a parish register. And yet St Peter's parish registers, beginning in 1570, are the oldest in Nottingham. The rector and churchwardens had been fined for not keeping the records and perhaps this had a salutary effect! The records are fascinating, so in 1624 for instance, St Peter's had 634 parishioners, which made up around a quarter of the town's total. The area was already quite built-up, but with open ground to the south, towards the River Leen. There are examples of unusual gifts made to the church such as by Luke Jackson in 1631. A prominent London merchant, Jackson was born in

Left: St Peter's Church exterior.

Below: St Peter's Church interior.

Above: St Peter's Church ancient font.

Right: Detail of carving at St Peter's Church.

Nottingham. He left £2 for the St Peter's rector to preach two sermons annually. These were one to commemorate the defeat of the Spanish Armada in 1588, and another to give thanks for deliverance from the 1605 Gunpowder Plot.

In 1640, the rector George Cotes died while giving a lengthy series of sermons on Jeremiah ch48, v13 (perhaps comparing the idolatry of Moab to what he saw in England), and this was reputed to be 'the longest sermon ever preached'. Cotes had Puritan sympathies, though he followed Archbishop Laud's instructions to celebrate communion in the sanctuary and behind the altar rails. This was instead of in the nave with his congregation all round and whilst some parishioners disagreed, they were called before the Archdeacon's Court for refusing communion in the new style. Such was the seriousness with which these matters were considered at that time.

There is much more to tell but space is limited. The nineteenth and twentieth centuries brought major changes to the town then city), to the communities, and to the church. A most significant alteration was the pastoral reorganisation in

2002 whereby the parish merged with All Saints', Raleigh Street, and then in 2004, St Peter's and All Saints' were joined to St Mary's to create a single city centre ministry. St Peter's is now into the twenty-first century with new facilities, and the church itself more accessible, physically and spiritually. The site and its church still have a strong sense of history and of purpose extending over more than 900 years.

16. King Charles House, King Charles Street

The house is named after the location nearby where King Charles I raised his standard to declare war on the Parliamentarians, in 1642. Nottingham was longstanding as a Royalist centre and with its strategic significance made a strong statement of intent.

The building includes Nos 3, 5 and 7 King Charles Street, Standard Hill, and most recently has been used for office premises. Built from 1810 to 1814, in red brick, with painted ashlar dressings, a slate roof, with rendered plinth, and

Above: King Charles House wall plate.

Left: King Charles House exterior.

King Charles Street road name and blue plaque.

modillion wooden eaves, it was tastefully altered in the late twentieth century. The house is three storied with windows of the second floor smaller than the ground and first floors, and all mostly original glazing with bar sashes, wedge lintels and double keystones. There is a symmetrical front to the building, small central windows flanked by larger ones, and a moulded, round-arched doorway with recessed six-panel door, and fanlight. It is Grade II listed and the overall effect is quite charming, and the location has its significant historical connections too.

17. Sheriff House, No. 64 St James's Street

St James's Street has several striking eighteenth-century houses, and of these the best by far is Sheriff House. There was formerly a datestone marked with 'C1767L' on this five-bay, three-storey house with its pedimented doorway with a Diocletian window and a pediment with ball finials. Sheriff House is very similar to Derby's No. 41 Friar Gate built in 1771 and it has been suggested that the architect was Joseph Pickford of that city. This wonderful building was constructed for Cornelius Launder who lived there from 1775 to 1806, and spared no expense on his own house. He was the High Sheriff of Nottingham in 1775, a noted landlord in the area, but also famously a miser, and this was where he lived until his death. Without rear gardens, these properties had separate plots called 'vistas' over the street. The other houses on the street include several of a similar vintage and though slightly younger, No. 76, was lived in by Lord Byron from 1798 to 1799.

Sold in 1908, until 1956 Sheriff House was the headquarters of the Medico-Chirurgical Society (which cultivates and promotes medical science, matters affecting the medical profession, and medical education) and it was then sold in 1990. The sale led to the 1995 restoration by Nicholas Forman Hardy and Gervase Jackson-Stops, and conversion to office usage.

Above left: Sheriff House, No. 64 St James's Street.

Above right: The front doorway of Sheriff House, No. 64 St James's Street.

18. No. 72 St James's Street

This Grade II listed building is described by Historic England as 'Number 72 and attached railings, 72, St James' Street' rather than simply Number 72; in other words, the railings are a significant part of the revised listing, and they too are needing preservation.

Pevsner described the property originally, and it is noted by Historic England in a detailed architectural listing as a town house, now offices, and with attached railings. It is late eighteenth century restored in the late twentieth, constructed of red brick, with painted ashlar basement and dressings, and a concrete tile roof with two gable stacks. There is a second-floor sill band, modillion eaves cornice and with triglyph frieze. The house is four storeys plus basement with a four-window range, the windows being glazing bar sashes. There is a rusticated stucco ground-floor arcade with an off-centre beaded panelled door and cast-iron fanlight, and windows with stucco scallops in the tympana. Outside of the frontage there are the wrought-iron railing and balustrade to steps, on a rendered plinth. The first floor has baluster panels and bands below the window, and the second floor has

No. 72 St James's Street.

similar windows on a sill band, whilst the third floor has smaller windows. These are all with panelled wedge lintels with double keystones. The rear of the building has a central, round-arched, half-glazed door plus fanlight, and this is flanked to the left by a sixteen-pane sash and to the right by a blank. There are two segmental light wells with wrought-iron railings. Above, there are two glazing bar sashes and a blank on each floor, all of these are segment-headed. There is a set-back single bay to the right with a round-arched ground-floor window. This an example of a meticulously detailed architectural description and this is significant in listing and protection. However, I do think it is equally important to simply say that this is a beautiful building, in an important setting, and absolutely irreplaceable.

19. Nottingham General Hospital, Postern Street

With its rising population, there was the demand in Nottingham for improved healthcare and hospitals. However, the early provision of hospitals or almshouses, for example, was often based on bequests and support from wealthy and enlightened philanthropists like Anne Burton. Originally, what care was available came from religious institutions, but Henry VIII largely ended that with the Dissolution. The workhouse, for example, which had replaced the old City Workhouse when the Victoria station was built, became the Bagthorpe Hospital

Above: Nottingham General Hospital, Postern Street.

Left: The former Nottingham General Hospital, Postern Street, now a children's nursery.

and then the City Hospital. However, by 1782, a dedicated general hospital was constructed. Fast-forward another 250 years and today Nottingham has one of the leading teaching hospitals in the country, the Queen's Medical Centre. This opened in 1970 as one of the largest hospitals in the UK, and indeed one of the biggest teaching hospitals in Europe, and it has expanded considerably since then.

So, as smaller settlements become towns and these grow as urban centres, then there is a need for health care and especially for centralised hospitals. Nottingham General Hospital was founded in 1782 and closed in 1992, the first properly constituted hospital in the city. In 1787, the hospital was extended with the opening of the Derbyshire wing. A third storey was built onto the original building in 1855.

20. Rotunda, Park Row

Another new wing on the Park Row frontage of the hospital was opened in 1879, and this was followed by the Jubilee Wing with its circular wards, which opened in 1900. The naming was in celebration of Queen Victoria's diamond jubilee. The design was the work of architect Alfred Waterhouse, who was also behind some of the most distinctive and expensive buildings of the Victorian period including

The Rotunda, Park Row, was once part of the hospital.

The Rotunda, Park Row, and now the Roundhouse Bar & Kitchen restaurant.

Manchester Town Hall and the London Natural History Museum. This now privately owned Grade II listed building was formerly part of the Nottingham General Hospital for more than a century. It was opened to care for patients undergoing surgery, and during the First World War wounded soldiers returning from the Western Front were sent there for recovery.

Today this is the Roundhouse Bar & Kitchen restaurant. Like many urban hospitality venues, this venture had a very difficult time during and following Covid-19 lockdown. However, it reopened with new owners in August 2023. The current vision is for it to be 'more of a bar serving food, than a restaurant'.

21. Ropewalk Pumping Station, the Ropewalk

The Ropewalk was an area or path where rope was manufactured from hemp. Several workers pulled and twisted the fibres whilst it was wrapped around a spool holding one end, whilst being drawn in a straight line. Close by but unconnected to the street name, on 30 July 1861, 5,000–10,000 people paid a shilling for gain admittance to the barracks to watch the tightrope walker Blondin perform on a high 'wire'. As Nottingham expanded, many of its citizens relied on pumped groundwater from artesian wells, and with primitive cesspit sewerage disposal this was a problem as it was in many towns and cities in the 1800s. The Ropewalk Pumping Station is a Grade II listed building, built along with a reservoir on Park Row by the Nottingham Waterworks Company in 1850. The station used a 60-hp (45-kW) Cornish beam engine to pump from two 240-ft-deep (73-m) wells to supply 960,000 imperial gallons (4,400,000 litres) of water per day.

However, location proved a problem when it was discovered that in this case the water was contaminated by effluent from Nottingham General Cemetery. Analysis in 1873, indicated that the water had 31.5 grains (2.04 g) of solid effluent per gallon, and the Ropewalk Pumping Station closed around 1880. The building was then used as a garage from 1930, subsequently became derelict. It has now been sensitively restored to a modern business use, although the nearby 'Ropewalk pub' has closed and is derelict.

Right: The Ropewalk Pumping Station, the Ropewalk, once run by Nottingham Waterworks Company.

Below: The Ropewalk Pumping Station, now business premises.

The Ropewalk Pub, Derby Road, now closed down.

22. Park Tunnel, the Park

Built in 1855, the Park Tunnel was intended to provide a direct route for horse-drawn carriages to the Park Estate from Derby Road in Nottingham. The area was once the private hunting park of the Duke of Newcastle, owner of Nottingham Castle mansion. So, in the 1830s, the 5th Duke retained the services of architect Thomas Chambers (T. C.) Hine (1813–99) to design and subsequently build the Park Tunnel. This was principally to provide a main entrance to the Park, whilst developing the surrounding area for wealthier residents. (Hine was also responsible later repairs to Nottingham Castle and its conversion to a museum.) This former carriage drive, connecting the Park Estate directly to Derby Road, is 125 metres long, and construction, which began in 1844, took eleven years.

The idea of a connecting tunnel from the grand villas being built straight to the Derby Road perhaps took hold with the designer of the houses, Peter Frederick Robinson, in the late 1820s. This area of the Park was left open for recreational and sports use, with, for instance, a timber-clad tennis pavilion. Thomas Winter was responsible for planning the venture in 1839, and the cutting through of the tunnel started in 1844. Completion of the project for the 5th Duke of Newcastle was by T. C. Hine in 1855 when he cut through 135 yards (125 metres) to include stairs leading from the central section to the Ropewalk. Terraced houses by the same architect stand above the tunnel, which once completed was considered too steep for use by carriages, but acceptable for those on foot. The tunnel is still in use by pedestrians today, providing access from Derby Road, Upper College Street and the Ropewalk to the Park. The tunnel emerges halfway along the Derby Road by what is now student accommodation. The house now above the tunnel was built later, in 1881. Overall, this is a remarkable and perhaps unique feature and one of Nottingham's very special places.

Right: Park Tunnel, the Park, showing the houses above.

Below: Park Tunnel, the Park, with steps down.

Park Tunnel, the Park, through the archway.

23. The Old Bluecoat School, Bluecoat Lane, off Mansfield Road

Charity schools, sometimes called blue coat schools, or simply the Blue School, were indeed significant in English educational history, built and maintained in various parishes supported by voluntary contributions of local inhabitants. They were initially established to teach poor children to read and write, and other aspects of education, and often maintained by religious organisations. The latter provided clothing and education to students freely or at little charge. In most charity schools, children were put out to trades, services, etc., by the same charitable foundation. Some schools were more ambitious and aimed to send a few pupils on to university. Still with a strongly religious ethos, the Blue Coat schools have evolved and developed into significant providers of education for young people.

The Old Bluecoat School on Mansfield Road is now the YMCA International Community Centre. The Bluecoat Charity School was founded in 1706 but this particular building (by the architect T. C. Hine) was built in 1852. The school moved here from its previous site in Weekday Cross in 1853, and it was relocated again in 1967, to its present site in Aspley Lane. It has broad mullion-and-transom windows and a projecting corner range with scroll gables and niches with statues of two Bluecoat scholars. These were copied from the ones in the original Jacobean building by J. Stonehouse. As the photographs show, the building and its immediate surroundings are presently in need of tender loving care!

Above left: The Old Bluecoats School, Bluecoat Lane, off Mansfield Road.

Above right: View of one of the statues at the Old Bluecoats School.

Below: The Old Bluecoats School street sign.

24. Castle Works, Castle Road

This imposing brick-built premises on Castle Road has a date stone marked AD 1900. Nikolaus Pevsner, writing about the buildings of Nottingham back in 1951, noted the importance and significance of some of the early to mid-Victorian industrial buildings especially warehouses. He comments on the imposing, brick-built constructions. In this particular case, the date is 1900 and so it falls between very late nineteenth century and the very early twentieth century. The wrought-iron gate is particularly imposing and the brickwork bears something of a nod to a decorative touch or two – the date stone with a coat of arms, for example.

Above left: Castle Works, Castle Road, ornamental gate and main entrance.

Above right: Castle Works, Castle Road, building frontage.

Left: Detail of the Castle Works wrought-iron gateway.

It is difficult to find detailed information on many of the old industrial buildings, but this seems to be at the junction of Castle Road and Park Street which became Park Boulevard when the River Leen was diverted in the 1800s. The gate bears the initials 'NC' and 'WW' which I take to be a reference to the Nottingham Castle Water Works or Nottingham Waterworks Company (back at least to the 1870s), though Historic England references 'Nottingham City Waterworks Building' but at the same site 'Nottingham Corporation Waterworks'.

It is Grade II listed building, and the list entry sheds rather more light on the detail and context. Known as Castle Works, Castle Boulevard it is the former corporation waterworks depot, is now offices. The attached railings are also listed. Dated 1900 it is of red brick, with ashlar dressings and slate and sheet metal roofs, with coped side wall stack and overall, in Flemish Renaissance Revival style with plinth and sill bands, and segment-arched openings with keystones. It is now converted into offices.

25. R. Chandler & Co., Alfred Street North

Known as the St Ann's Factories, Chandler's was at the apex of Alfred Street North and St Ann's Hill Road. The smaller factory a men's clothing manufacturer, called Wright and Co., and in the 1960s was run by Mr Beverely Wright who also had a small shop at Bulwell Marketplace, called, appropriately, 'Beverely's'. By 1972, the Chandler's building appears to have been the 'Raywarp factory' and further down the road were Alfred Street, Kilbourn Street, and Vicarage Street. (From nostalgic memories, lentontimes.co.uk.) The Mechanics Pub was on the opposite side of the street.

This massive Victorian building is a remarkable and imposing structure although it seems to not be listed by Historic England, but both main building and the factory adjacent appear to have been converted to contemporary usage. This former lace factory and the two buildings that follow next are part of Nottingham's rich post-industrial heritage and individually are both distinctive and unique. Such acute corner plot buildings often follow and mark out the former agricultural field patterns and the ownership of land at the time these areas were being urbanised. With pressure for space in the rapidly expanding township, you constructed your building to fit the land shape available rather than today's often rigid steel-girder framed boxes. This generates distinctive, never-to-be-repeated, irreplaceable buildings.

Chandler & Co., Alfred Street North, view of main building.

Chandler & Co., Alfred Street North, lower buildings.

Chandler & Co. street sign.

26. Nos 126–28 Derby Road

Built in 1877 by Richard Charles Sutton for E. C. Patchitt, a chemist, this landmark Nottingham building at Nos 126–28 Derby Road has, in its past, been a Boots chemist, a post office, and a popular restaurant. The architect Richard Sutton went on to design a various churches, warehouses, factories, and other commercial premises in Nottingham. His schemes included Jesse Boot's first purpose-built premises. E. C. Patchitt was noted in the records as a 'chemist and druggist' based at No. 128 Derby Road. There was a Robert Pullman, draper, at Nos 124 and 126, with John Arwenn German, wholesale tea and coffee dealer and family grocer, at No. 122. Thomas Taylor, tobacconist, was at No. 116 and Henry Allwood, butcher, at No. 114 Derby Road. There was William Hodges, boot and shoemaker, at Nos 110 and 112. This was clearly a vibrant commercial location.

By 1898–99 the records show Robert Henry Beverley, chemist and wine merchant, at No. 128, with Marigold Manufacturing Co., and a 'Branch Post, Telegraph and Money Order Office' with, by 1901, Nos 126–28 Derby Road noted as a post office. Robert Beverley, along with being a chemist and wine merchant was also the postmaster. His family were heavily involved too with wife Kate listed and their son Thomas (chemist's assistant) and daughter Bertha (post office clerk). By 1915 Nos 118 to 124 were a single property. Nos 126 and 128, the chemists, was now taken over as Boots Cash Chemists (Eastern) Limited.

In 1973, Ben Bowers restaurant was opened in the visually prominent corner building, offering menus from around the world. Having been very popular with its distinctive style, Ben Bowers eventually closed and became the '1877' bar, based on the year of construction, but this too closed and the handsome, bow-fronted property went into decline. However, it now has a new identity as a shop and student flats with plans by Paul Butler Associates, and the current retail unit is vintage emporium 'Happy Sunday Vintage' described a technicolour, rummagers' dream of vintage clothing, rare antique finds, one-of-a-kind mid-century furniture, and homeware. This is an iconic building that dominates the aesthetic as you come into Nottingham along Derby Road and is a significant part of Nottingham's rich built heritage. It is Grade II listed and described as French Renaissance Revival style.

Nos 126–28 Derby Road, built in 1877.

27. Nos 1 and 2 Barrack Lane, Derby Road

At Barrack Lane, off Derby Road, a mix of different residential properties now lines both sides of the old road, originally an open track leading up to Nottingham's only army barracks. In medieval times, in the absence of formal barracks, military troops stationed in a town had the entitlement to take up residence in any suitable buildings even if their owners objected. This situation led to considerable local resentment and so in 1689, a royal proclamation reduced the choice of accommodation to the inns alone. However, whilst innkeepers were obligated to take such 'guests' they were frequently not happy about it. So, in 1792 in Nottingham the new barracks were built. This was a sizeable undertaking with officers' quarters, a large block with over eighty rooms and barrack rooms for ordinary soldiers, a small hospital and surgery, a suttling house for provisions and supplies, a magazine for explosives, and stabling for three troops of horse. The excavated rubble for the site was taken to fill in the medieval fishponds in the park.

During the late 1700s and into the mid-1800s, the soldiers here were used to quell politically motivated riots, and so troops were brought in from distant towns, so they were not too familiar and friendly with the local communities. This was a governmental ploy used in major towns and cities across the country, and even apply more recently in the police deployments during the 1980s miners' strikes. By the 1850s, the conditions in army barracks generally were mostly described as wretched, with overcrowding, poor sanitation, and little ventilation. Married quarters were almost non-existent with couples merely sharing a bed in the barrack room corner and any children sleeping with them. There were attempts to limit to a maximum of six married men per hundred soldiers, with wives of 'unapproved' marriages forced to live separately from their husbands in lodgings elsewhere. In 1860, the 11th Hussars moved to new quarters in Burnley and the Army shifted its East Midlands Command to Sheffield. The barracks were never again used for permanent accommodation but just for troops passing through Nottingham on their way elsewhere, and in a few years were totally demolished.

The present building on the angle of Barrack Lane and Derby Road is yet another of Nottingham's hidden gems with a remarkable brick turret at the apex. The brickwork is very plain and today the property mixes accommodation to the first floor and retail on the ground floor facing Derby Road. The house numbers along Barrack Lane are, to say the least, difficult to fathom as they mix Barrack Lane numbers with those fronting the main road on one side and Western Terrace or Pelham Road on the other. By the late 1970s or 1980s, the corner shop was Park Batteries selling car batteries. The building dates from a little after 1833 as the land was advertised for sale for building in that year. 'A corner piece lying between the Derby Road and the Carriage Road leading to the Barracks, about 680 sq. yds. Desirable situation, commanding extensive views over Vale of Trent,

Nos 1 and 2 Barrack Lane, Derby Road.

also towards Wollaton Hall and combining advantages of The Park situation'. A quick look over the areas suggests that whilst the Barracks were undoubtedly demolished, some features of the various structures probably still remain, or at the very least, stonework and bricks have been reused.

28. No. 2 Alberta Terrace, off Sherwood Rise

In Victorian Nottingham, as elsewhere at the time, the problems of the sick, old, infirm, or abandoned were growing and the answer was the 'workhouse'. However, space was a growing challenge, and the Nottingham Union operated a number of scattered 'Homes for pauper children' including No. 4 Alberta Terrace, off Sherwood Rise. The property appears to have been demolished and more recently replaced by late twentieth-century houses. However, No. 2 Alberta Terrace remains and is included as an example of another of the hidden gems in many cases of ordinary housing with remarkable ornamentation.

Above: No. 2 Alberta Terrace, off Sherwood Rise.

Left: The ornate doorway of No. 2 Alberta Terrace.

A walk down Alberta Terrace also shows another trend of the later twentieth century, which is the loss of once ubiquitous corner shops with most converted to residences.

29. Norris Ladies Home (Almshouses), Berridge Road, Sherwood Rise

Erected in 1893, the Norris Ladies Home on Berridge Road, Sherwood Rise, is one of the lesser-known buildings of the Victorian Nottingham architect Watson Fothergill. The Norris Almshouses building stands at the end of Berridge Road and comprises a row of eight one-bedroom houses for ladies, designed by the architect Fothergill Watson and paid for by Mary Smith Norris (1827–1909). The dedication as the 'Norris Ladies Home' in 1893, was in memory of Mary's brother, John Norris. The charity's objectives were to 'provide a residence available for poor widows or spinsters, or for married couples of not less than sixty years of age, and resident in the City of Nottingham, or within a distance of six miles therefrom. Preferences shall be given to persons so qualified who are members of the Church of England or of some orthodox Protestant dissenting denomination'.

Norris Almshouses, Berridge Road, Sherwood Rise.

Above left: Norris Almshouses, through the gate.

Above right: Example of the building detail on Norris Almshouses.

30. No. 20 Park Terrace, off the Ropewalk

Pevsner in 1951 noted that any selection of Nottingham's Victorian buildings is to a large degree arbitrary, so that is the case. The choice of No. 20 Park Terrace is merely as an example of the type of building that took place from the early 1800s to the early 1900s, in and around or overlooking the once great medieval park associated with Nottingham Castle. Pevsner suggests that the Park was laid out after 1850, and certainly from 1854 onwards, under the influence of Nash in London's Regent's Park scattering large villas at generous distances. He suggests that Nottingham Park was less generous in its spacing and reflected Gothic and

No. 20 Park Terrace, off the Ropewalk.

No. 20 Park Terrace number plate.

Tudor detail in much of its design. Whilst he criticises the way the properties are packed into the landscape, he notes the importance in terms of the history of modern 'urbanism'. He also praises the elements of Victorian Picturesque too. There are significant buildings across all of this area and indeed along Lenton Road too, but space does not allow a more detailed comment.

31. HMP Nottingham, Gatehouse, Perry Road, Sherwood

HM Prison Nottingham (Perry Road, Sherwood) is a Category B men's prison, located in the Sherwood area of Nottingham. It was opened in 1890 and is operated by Her Majesty's Prison Service. The exterior buildings include the old gatehouse at Nottingham Prison, exterior offices and chapel, and the various wings. There is a huge exterior wall and a sign saying it is an offence to help prisoners escape, which I thought was a little obvious!

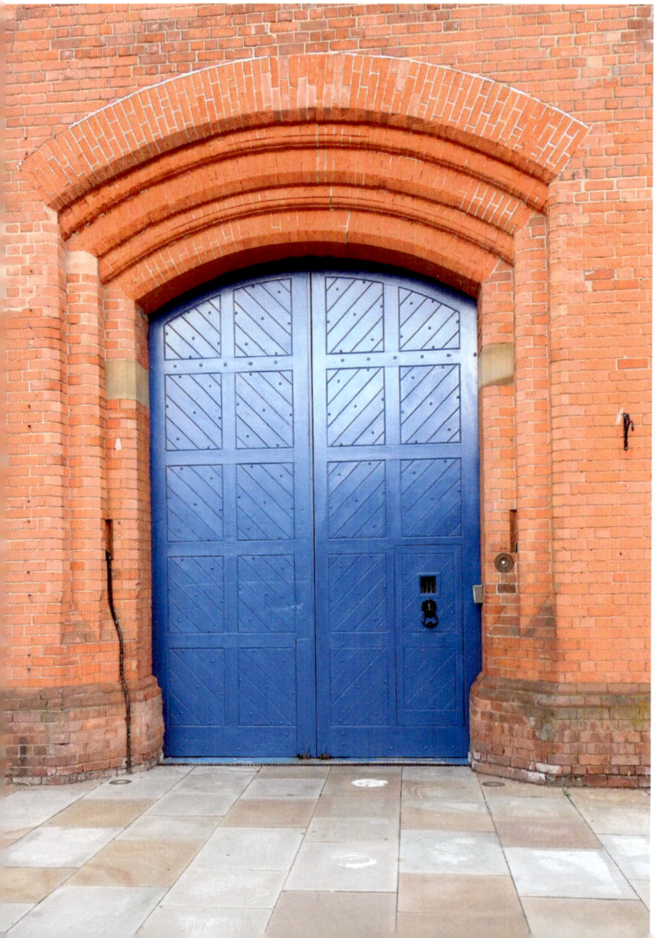

Above: Nottingham Prison main gatehouse, Perry Road, Sherwood.

Left: Nottingham Prison's main gateway and entrance.

The massive external wall of Nottingham Prison.

32. No. 10 Low Pavement

Low Pavement remains one of the most charming streets in old Nottingham. No. 10 (although it seems that the street number is not clearly shown anywhere) Low Pavement is a very ornate and interesting Grade II listed building, designed and built by Alfred Smith. It is a dramatic building on one of Nottingham's architecturally most interesting streets. Above No. 10, No. 12 Low Pavement is a stunning Victorian, five-bayed stuccoed house, whilst below, No. 8 by A. R. Calvert and formerly Café Uno, is Gothic inspired from 1903. The design of

Close-up of No. 10 Low Pavement's Gothic Revival window.

Above left: No. 10 Low Pavement.

Above right: No. 8 Low Pavement, formerly Café Uno.

No. 10 is robustly Gothic Revival and sports granite shafts plus foliage capitals to the strongly dominant oriel window. The whole vision is strongly influenced by Gothic Revivalist, architect, William Burges. Designed for office use, in 1992 was converted into restaurant, and is now vacant.

33. The Star Brewery, Radford Road

Many local and regional breweries have closed in recent decades, though there has been a rebound with the emergence of local distinction with microbreweries and craft brewers. Major cities like Nottingham often had several breweries that emerged and grew during the 1800s and 1900s to supply the expanding thirst of the centre's population of workers in the new factories. The local pubs and working men's clubs also became the centrepieces of much of the local social life, and distinctive local brews were at the heart of the experience. However, by the turn of the new millennium, the patterns changed, and the combination of cheaper bottled beers to drink at home, rising prices of beers in pubs, and growing awareness of the health hazards of smoking in public places meant fewer people were drinking in such establishments as pubs. The latter, and the banning of smoking in pubs, meant pub landlords faced a reduction in the amount of income they could generate. Closure of the big factories across the city and the region also took away local demand for a drinking haven after work or at the weekend. The consequences of these changes have meant both the demise of many breweries and the closure of pubs, compounded during Covid-19 lockdowns. A further trend has been for locally distinct, profitable breweries to be taken over by the big corporates, asset-stripped for their brands, the production centralised, and then the local breweries closed down. These are not trends peculiar to Nottingham but a national pattern almost everywhere.

One of Nottingham's most famous and distinctive brews was that founded by James Shipstone in 1852 at the Star Brewery in New Basford. They produced the Shipstones brand of beer, locally known as 'Shippos', and the distinctive illuminated red star at the top of the brewery's tower was a landmark that could be seen for miles around. The business thrived and expanded so that by 1939 the company owned nearly 600 licensed premises, thirty diesel lorries for long-distance delivery work, and fifty horses for local delivery work. The brewery remained

Star Brewery, Radford Road, main building.

Above: Star Brewery with the famous 'star' symbol.

Left: Star Brewery's unique clock.

an independent family business until 1978 when the company was purchased by Greenall's of Warrington, but as described earlier the long-term decline set in, and all brewing on site ended in 1991. However, as so often is the case, the brand was saved and there is now Shipstone's Beer Company Ltd operating from the Little Star Brewery, Old Basford, and described as 'A microbrewery producing local beers that have been around since 1852. Set up to preserve and protect our local brewing heritage, we brew a range of quality cask ales from recipes found in the archives. The range of real ale has something for everyone from a traditional bitter, an English IPA, a pale ale and a smooth nut brown ale. Now back to award winning ways we are proud that we have changed perceptions and taking the name back to the right place that James Shipstone's deserves. Once a proud sponsor of Nottingham Forest, Shipstone's is a local household name that we feel is heritage worth handing down.' Of course, there is a danger that as the new business grows and becomes more profitable the brewing and hospitality giants will once again step in…

At the Star Brewery site, the company offices have been taken over, with some housing and retail units on other parts of the site. Presently owned by a local auction house, the landmark Victorian building built in 1900 still stands.

34. Waverley Building, Nottingham Trent University, Waverley Street

In 1836, the Government Select Committee on Art and Manufactures produced a report highlighting concerns about the standard of design in the industry. Higher standards abroad forced manufacturers to buy or copy foreign designs. Later in 1836, the Board of Trade established the Government School of Design in London, where, in 1837, it was opened at Somerset House. To encourage practical art in other populous areas of Britain, a Government School of Design was then established in each of several provincial towns. These were placed where manufacturing industries were already in existence. Inevitably, the original title was adjusted to include the name of the town where it was located, whilst locally, simply being referred to as, 'the School of Design'. In Nottingham, the School of Design opened on 1 April 1843 at the People's Hall, Beck Lane (now Heathcote Street), moving to Plumptre House in Stoney Street in 1852, and to Commerce Square, off High Pavement, in 1858. In 1863, a site was purchased in Waverley Street for the construction of a building specifically for the school which ultimately became the Art College of Nottingham Trent University.

Building work started on 23 May 1863, but the foundation stone wasn't laid until 22 October that year when Henry Pelham-Clinton, 5th Duke of Newcastle, was available for the ceremony. The school, designed by architect Frederick Bakewell, was opened by Henry Pelham-Clinton, 6th Duke of Newcastle, on 19 June 1865. In front of the building is a statue of the artist Richard Parkes Bonington, produced by Watson Fothergill.

The Waverley Building, Waverley Street.

Left: Detail of the carved keystone on the Waverley Building.

Below: The Waverley Building's ornamental coat of arms.

35. Watson Fothergill's Office, Nos 15–17 George Street

This elegant building, constructed in 1895, was the headquarters of eminent architect Watson Fothergill, a man who left a huge legacy of richly designed buildings in the city of Nottingham. It is interesting to observe a working building designed by an architect for their own personal use, rather than one constructed for a client. The offices of Nottingham architect, Watson Fothergill were at Nos 15–17 George Street and are now a Grade II listed building and converted in the late twentieth century, it is now a solicitor's office. The Gothic Revival two-storey building with attics is, as might be expected, especially striking with elaborate polychrome features, red brick with ashlar and blue brick dressings, and with a plain tile roof with tile crests. There are stylised brick gable and side-wall stacks, blue-brick plinth and first-floor band. The front has a five-window range, with windows of mostly wooden-framed, cross-casements, plain sashes, and leaded glazing. The asymmetrical front has a board door with a shouldered

Above: Watson Fothergill's Office, with ornate bay window.

Right: Watson Fothergill's Office, Nos 15–17 George Street.

opening with shafts, and then two segmental arches with a grey granite column, with now a modern panelled door and window. There is a further basket-arched passage entrance and a two-light window with plate tracery. There is a machicolated turret (a mock defensive structure for dropping stones or perhaps boiling oil onto would-be attackers below a castle wall but obviously not in this case!) with three trefoil-headed windows with gables. The octagonal spire roof with two steep-pitched, hipped lucarnes, with crests and finial. Four trefoil-headed windows have clustered shafts. There are figures such as a medieval architect, and busts of figures such as English architect, designer, artist, and critic Augustus Welby Northmore Pugin, notable for his pioneering development of the Gothic Revival style of architecture. There is another of George Edmund Street RA (1824–81), also known as G. E. Street, an architect from Woodford, Essex, and another champion of Gothic Revivalism. There is much more detail on close inspection both inside and out, but overall the building shows Fothergill's eclectic style with its figures and inscriptions a homage to his architectural inspirations, and absolutely unique.

The elaborate windows and statue of Watson Fothergill's Office.

36. Nottingham Cemetery, Canning Terrace, off Talbot Street

This is an Anglican cemetery of 1836 with a Dissenters' extension added in 1865, both with their own mortuary chapels, and both since demolished. The cemetery was set up by the Nottingham General Cemetery Company, established by a special Act of Parliament given royal assent in 1836. The original site was made up of 14 acres (*c.* 6ha) with an additional 4 acres (*c.* 1.6ha) added under the 1845 Enclosure Act and shown on the Enclosure Award map (1865). The latter enclosed fields and meadows used to graze the animals of the city burgesses or freeholders. To compensate for the loss under the award of open land formerly used for recreation, space was allocated for public amenity and recreation and public walks. There were 130 acres (*c.* 54ha) to include Queen's Walk, Queen's Walk Park (Meadows Cricket Ground), Victoria Park, Robin Hood Chase, Corporation Oaks, St Ann's Hill (Belle Vue Reservoir), Elm Avenue, Nottingham Arboretum, Waterloo Promenade, the Church Cemetery, the Forest, and the General Cemetery, created as public open spaces from the enclosures.

With a growing urban population and the high mortality rates of Victorian townships, the demand for the cemetery's facilities was great and expanding. So, by 1923, there had been 150,000 bodies buried, leading the then Medical Officer of Health to be concerned about the cemetery's future if this scale of interments was maintained. With this in mind, a further bill was brought to Parliament by Nottingham Corporation to close the cemetery should more interments take place unless they were in existing family graves. By the mid-twentieth century, the operational costs were escalating and in the post-Second World War period the Nottingham General Cemetery Company approached the Corporation to take on responsibility of the cemetery. However, the Corporation declined, leading the Company into voluntary liquidation, and the cemetery being vested in the Crown Estate. Subsequently, in 1956, the Crown Estate passed the site freehold and associated responsibilities to the City Council. This is indeed a pattern familiar to many twentieth-century towns and cities because once a cemetery is 'full' and there can be no further new burial plots, there is no regular income-stream and the private company goes bankrupt, with responsibility ultimately passing to the local authority and the site reverting to an open space but with historic overtones. The site is a Grade II listed 'park and garden'.

The principal entrance is from Canning Terrace at the top of Wollaton Street at the south-west boundary of the cemetery. The cemetery gatehouse is itself a Grade II listed building designed by S. S. Rawlinson for the General Cemetery Company. It was built with a symmetrical I from 1837 to 1840 in stucco and brick with slate roofs and corniced stacks. The square gatehouse is flanked by

Entrance to Nottingham Cemetery, Derby Road.

sets of almshouses having pedimented centres. The main processional route leads from the gates (by Falconer and Company of Derby, 1839) and gatehouse, north-east along a raised route to where the Anglican mortuary chapel (demolished late 1950s) once stood. Both chapels on site were in a dangerous state by the 1950s and were subsequently demolished. The extensive site has marked walkways and both graves and monuments relating to past inhabitants of the city, and now mature trees fulfilling its twenty-first-century role as public greenspace.

Finally, the General Cemetery includes the war graves of 336 Commonwealth service personnel and one Belgian war grave from the First World War and ten from the Second World War. These were mainly dead from the wartime military hospitals in and around Nottingham. Around a hundred graves are from the First World War and in a special war graves plot with a commemorative wall listing the names of the fallen. The Commonwealth War Graves Commission now maintains these graves.

37. Theatre Royal, Upper Parliament Street

Entertainment, leisure, and culture are at the heart of towns and cities and always have been. The Theatre Royal in Nottingham, England, is a theatrical venue in the heart of Nottingham city centre and owned by Nottingham City Council and is part of a complex that includes the city's Royal Concert Hall. A keystone of the city's cultural activities, the Theatre Royal attracts major touring dramas, opera, ballet, West End musicals, and an annual pantomime.

The venue's history extends back over 150 years to when Nottingham Theatre Company was established and owned by lace manufacturers John and William Lambert. Under their guidance, the Theatre Royal was completed in 1865 after six months of work and costing around £15,000, opening in September 1865, with Sheridan's *The School for Scandal*. The classic façade and Corinthian columns designed by Charles J. Phipps are still a major Nottingham landmark. In 1897, the leasing arrangements changed with a different lessee, the newly formed limited company Robert Arthur Theatres Ltd, which had theatres in both England and Scotland. The new company presented a wide range of acclaimed plays, opera, revues, and pantomimes until running out of funds in 1912. At this juncture, the chairman and founder of Howard & Wyndham Ltd, Michael Simons, became chairman of the Robert Arthur group. The Arthur theatres were now operated under the same directors and managers as Howard & Wyndham. However, when the long lease ended in 1924 the theatre was bought outright by Moss Empires.

The theatre has had many important shows and impacted on the national theatrical scene. For example, Baroness Orczy's *The Scarlet Pimpernel* (1903) was first produced at the Theatre Royal by Fred Terry and Julia Neilson before the story of the play was published as a novel. Interestingly, the play began with little interest or success, but the later novel influenced the 'mystery genre' and

Above: Theatre Royal, Upper Parliament Street.

Right: Theatre Royal, with a side view of the main frontage.

arguably created the 'masked hero' idea which has evolved since then to much bigger things. In October 1952, the theatre made history with the world premiere of *The Mousetrap* as part of a pre-West End tour. The London West End play went on to become the longest-running theatrical production in the world. Two years later, William Douglas Home's comedy *The Manor of Northstead* also premiered before transferring to the West End. However, despite the successes, by the later twentieth century, the theatre was in dire need of restoration. Indeed, it had a reputation as one of Britain's worst theatres for backstage conditions and facilities for the cast. So, in 1969, the City Council bought the theatre and began a major restoration costing £4 million. Completed in 1978, the Theatre Royal was officially reopened by Princess Anne on 6 June 1978, and the venue continues to stage hugely successful events and performances.

38. Royal Concert Hall, South Sherwood Street

Nottingham Royal Concert Hall is owned by Nottingham City Council and is part of a complex in a prestigious city centre location that also includes the city's Theatre Royal. The site of Nottingham's Royal Concert Hall was previously the old Empire Palace of Varieties which was designed and built by Frank Matcham in 1898. However, the Empire Palace finally closed in 1958 and the building was demolished in 1969 to make way for a road-widening scheme.

Nevertheless, it was clear that an upgraded replacement was needed, and the client for such a project was Nottingham City Council. Work on the Royal Concert Hall began in 1980 and was completed in 1982, providing Nottingham with a contemporary 2,499-seater auditorium. The first artist to perform there, back in November 1982, was Elton John. Costing £12 million to complete, the Royal Concert Hall's striking modern architecture has proved to be a city landmark at the heart of Nottingham City centre. The 1980s purpose-built facility

Royal Concert Hall, South Sherwood Street.

Royal Concert Hall with its distinctive overshot front.

was designed by the Renton Howard Wood Levin Partnership (architects of both the Sheffield Crucible Theatre, and Manchester's Bridgewater Hall), and it has proved to be spectacularly successful.

39. Lenton Hurst, off Beeston Lane

This spectacular property is a part of the University Park Campus of the University of Nottingham. Associated with the more modern Lenton Hall accommodation, Lenton Hurst was designed in what is described as handsome Arts and Crafts style by Marshall & Turner for W. G. Player in 1896. The property also has a garden by the eminent garden designer Gertrude Jekyll. Created in 1911, it is a sunken garden with formal geometric style and a rock garden terrace separating it from the house above. W. G. or William Goodacre Player was one of the two sons of the Saffron Waldron-born Nottingham entrepreneur John Player, who had come to the town in 1862 at the age of twenty-three years. Having started out in the drapery business he moved into agricultural products such as manure and seeds, with loose tobacco as a sideline. However, it was the tobacco business which took off to the point that John Player's cigarettes were to become a globally recognised household name. By the late 1800s, the two sons of John Player, William Goodacre and John Dane became the owners and managing directors of

Above: Lenton Hurst, University of Nottingham, view of house and garden.

Left: Lenton Hurst, University of Nottingham, view of the bay windows from the garden.

John Player & Sons Ltd, the Nottingham-based cigarette empire. It was William that built Lenton Hurst, having submitted plans to Nottingham City Council in 1896 to build a private residence on Adam's Hill, Derby Road. William and his wife Mabel lived there for thirty years. William did acquire a site at Ednaston near Brailsford, Derbyshire, where he had a spectacular property built to a design by Sir Edwin Lutyens and which, when completed in 1914, was described as 'the most perfect country house that Lutyens designed'. However, Mabel did not like it and the couple remained at Lenton Hurst, before finally relocating to Whatton Manor near Bingham. William lived there until 1959 when he died at the age of ninety-three, leaving an estate worth nearly £2 million. His longevity poses a question, for me, at a least: did he smoke?

40. Alton's Cigar Factory, Nos 154–62 Derby Road

This nineteenth-century cigar factory at Nos 154–62 Derby Road was the combination of several eighteenth- and nineteenth-century houses. The properties, including a late eighteenth-century home, were converted in 1897 to 1898 by Frederick Ball & Lamb to become Alton's Cigar Factory. Then, for more than a century, E. Alton & Co. were manufactures of top-class Havana tobacco cigars for the likes of shops such as Harrods and Selfridges. Customers reputedly included the late Sir Winston Churchill and they were thus a central feature of his wartime image and persona. This may not actually be the case as he was said to prefer the genuine 'Havana' cigars made in Cuba, whereas these were cigars were made with Havana tobacco but in Nottingham. The firm was originally established in 1862 by Edmund Alton above a music shop in Chapel Bar. As the business prospered and grew, it moved to Peveril Street, and then, in 1897, to the Derby Road site. The latter was a building once used as a private waterworks pumping water from an artesian well which sold water to subscribers in the Park and surrounding areas. The early twentieth-century factory employed about 130 people at its peak, producing an output of over a million cigars every year. However, when due to falling demand the factory was closed in 1992, this was the last small cigar-making factory left in Britain.

Following closure, the factory, Victorian shop, and neighbouring townhouses in 2003 were developed by Boden Associates architects into luxury city centre apartments linked with the new Canning Circus building. The factory and shop, both Grade II listed, were derelict for a long time with whole sections of floor missing, supporting walls badly damaged and the roof collapsed in places. The state of the buildings meant they were unsafe to survey and considering the importance of the buildings to Nottingham's architectural heritage and of course their protected status, this was a major challenge for those planning the project. A key aspiration was to respect the building's listed status and to retain essential features of the original structure. However, by 2024, whilst the ground-floor shop was used by a letting agency, the frontage of the main former Georgian building was looking decidedly rundown and sad.

Left: Alton's Cigar Factory, Nos 154–62 Derby Road.

Below: Alton's Cigar Factory, now a letting agency.

41. Queen's Chambers, King Street

This very distinctive property is a Grade II listed building on the corner of Long Row and King Street. In 1897, Queen's Chambers was built in the Tudor Revival Gothic style to a design by local architect Fothergill Watson and in fact one of his most prominent buildings. The work was for wine merchant Edward Skipwith, who had long had a wine-selling business in premises on Long Row. This dramatic building of four shops with offices on the floors above, was a retirement project and perhaps as an investment. More recently, in 1993, Queen's Chambers was refurbished by architect Thomas Fish at a cost of around £500,000. The work took six months, and the project won the Lord Mayor's Urban Design Award in 1993.

Queen's Chambers, King Street.

42. The Trent Building, University of Nottingham, Jubilee Avenue

Educational institutions, particularly universities, are now at the very core of modern cities and are often the heartbeat of their social and economic functions. University College Nottingham was initially opened in 1881, originally on Shakespeare Street, and for the town, having a major and prestigious university was a mark of both status and aspiration. However, by the 1920s, inspired by the North American campus model of universities, and to an extent mirroring Birmingham in the West Midlands, Nottingham also developed ambitions for a major campus for its academic institution. The influential Nottingham businessman and philanthropist Jesse Boot, 1st Baron Trent, had transformed into a national retailer: the local The Boots business that his father, John Boot, had founded. Boots was rebranded as 'Chemists to the Nation', and Jesse Boot was anxious that in a similar style, the University of Nottingham might become the University of the East Midlands. He consequently purchased Highfields, Lenton House, and Lenton

Trent Building, University of Nottingham.

Above left: Trent Building, entrance to the quadrangle.

Above right: The Trent Building's clock tower.

Hall, to make these the basis for a new university vision. His original plan had been to relocate his business there and for himself to reside at Lenton House, but his wife objected and refused to leave their home at The Park. So instead, Boot and his architect Percy Morley Horder, set about designing their vision of a new university campus. This included Highfields Lake being enlarged and the lands around it drained, and the Trent Building (named after its benefactor Lord Trent), at University Park becoming the university's central administrative hub.

The Trent Building was constructed from 1922 to 1928 and is described as classicist in Portland stone with a giant Roman Doric and a tall clock tower. The campus evolved over subsequent decades as the university expanded, and this was generally in accord with 1920's vision. To me the effect is spectacular, but can feel rather cold and heartless, but that is merely my opinion. The Nottinghamshire writer D. H. Lawrence was not too impressed and once described the building as looking like an 'iced cake'. The University of Nottingham is both a Russell Group member and a red-brick university.

43. Council House, Long Row

For industrial cities emerging during the 1800s and 1900s, their influence, power and prestige were reflected in corporate buildings and related ventures. This may be difficult to recollect with today's slimline, cut-down local councils with their stripped-down budgets, but they had grand buildings designed to be both functional and to showcase corporate status. This prestigious building was designed by the Corporation's in-house architect, T. Cecil Howitt, and built around 1926 to 1929. The Council House is a key landmark of Nottingham's commercial heartland, with a shopping arcade at the centre, and the council offices running along the west front. The idea of rebuilding or replacing the old Exchange had been considered ever since the turn of the nineteenth century, but it was not until the 1920s that the scheme took hold in earnest. Apparently, in 1923, the chairman of the Corporation's Estates Committee, Herbert Bowles, came across the young architect T. Cecil Howitt working late on ideas and projects. They chatted and smoked, and consequently, Bowles offered the young housing designer the chance to develop his ideas for the replacement building for the old Exchange premises. The plans emerged for a centre based around a top-end shopping arcade based on or inspired by Milan's Galleria Vittorio Emanuele, under a dome somewhat like St Paul's Cathedral. This was also to incorporate into the complex the existing bank and offices, and the Corporation's councillors demanded that a mayoral suite and a grand chamber were added to the plans. When news emerged of the acceptance of this design there were grumbles from independent architects that they had not been asked to submit their own plans, ideas, and designs. However, this was the era of very affluent and powerful

Council House, Long Row and Market Square.

Above: Council House, view of the imposing front.

Right: The Council House's dome.

local authorities and the strongly classical design presented by Howitt in 1924, was accepted. Building went ahead and was completed in 1929, when it was formally opened by the Prince of Wales on 2 May.

44. Cripps Hall, University of Nottingham, Lenton Hall Drive

Cripps Hall for men was a gift to the University of Nottingham from the benefactor, Sir Cyril Cripps (Sir Cyril Humphrey Cripps DL, 1915–2000),

Above: Cripps Hall, University of Nottingham.

Left: Cripps Hall's main entrance.

an English businessman and a philanthropist. Humphrey Cripps was educated at Northampton School for Boys and then studied Natural Sciences at St John's College, Cambridge. He went on to head and diversify the family business interests and was heavily involved in the family's charitable activities through the Cripps Foundation. This charity was established in 1956 by the Cripps family and subsequently made major donations to universities, colleges, schools, churches, hospitals, and museums. Amongst these gifts was that of the Cripps Hall of Residence at University Park, Nottingham. The building was completed in 1959, and Cripps went on to support other major facilities across the campus. In its elegant setting in a leafy campus with broad tree-lined avenues, this is a Grade II listed building. Cripps Hall was designed by Farquaharson, McMorran & Whitby, and endowed by Cyril Thomas Cripps. The structure is described as Renaissance Revival style with a Great Hall, a square clock-tower, and quadrangles.

45. Newton Building, Nottingham Trent University, Burton Street

Nottingham's original university college began life in the Arkwright Building in 1877 to 1881, and this led to the establishment of the University of Nottingham, with a full academic university charter granted in 1948. At that time, the now university, ceded the Arkwright Building to the fledgling Technical College,

Newton Building, Nottingham Trent University, Burton Street.

and the Newton Building on Burton Street was ultimately developed to replace it. Designed by Charles Hyde (T. Cecil Howitt & Partners), the building was completed from 1956 to 1958, and described as a modern 'slab and podium' style, which might now be interpreted as 'blocky modernist'. The entrance area has pilasters to the front and the eight-storey 'slab' has striking strip windows. In 1970, the College of Technology merged with the College of Art and Design to form Trent Polytechnic, and then, like many similar institutions nationally, in 1992, the Polytechnic was granted full university status (i.e., its own charter and the power to award degrees), as Nottingham Trent University. This became one of the now many emerging 'new' new universities.

46. The Hole in the Wall, North Sherwood Street

This is a 1930s art deco building, and according to the wall plaque, there was an original pub on the site that dated from around 1860. Not large, this was claimed to have a total capacity of eleven people. However, the latter is suggested to be an urban myth or else a marketing ploy since the nineteenth-century maps don't show a public house here. It may also be a case of confusion with nearby

The Hole in the Wall public house, North Sherwood Street.

Duke of St Albans formerly on Sherwood Street but demolished in 1963. The latter was reputed to be Nottingham's smallest public house. The Hole in the Wall is a popular venue, has been enlarged, and is therefore slightly more spacious. It is now registered as an Asset of Community Value.

The name of the pub is suggested to derive from maybe a snug corner, near the town walls, or somehow from a hole made in the wall of the debtors' prisons or similar institutions and through which prisoners received money, meat, or other charitable donations. However, there is no obvious evidence to support such stories.

47. Nottingham Playhouse, Park Row, off Maid Marion Way

Nottingham is well provided for in terms of theatre and other entertainment, and of course this includes Nottingham Playhouse. Built from 1961 to 1963, the current venue was opened in 1963, having been first established as a repertory theatre in 1948 in the former Goldsmith Street cinema. Indeed, Nottingham Playhouse has been one of the United Kingdom's leading production theatres since its foundation in 1948. Touring work nationally and internationally, the Playhouse remains firmly rooted in its vibrant home city, where its spacious modernist building, fronted by Anish Kapoor's Sky Mirror, is one of the region's most popular landmarks. The Playhouse is considered one of central Nottingham's most significant, twentieth century buildings. The funding initially came from a fortunate windfall of compensation to the council on the nationalisation of its gas works. However, the decision to fund the project was hotly debated and this delayed the construction. The architect chosen was a man called Peter Moro, and his design has been the

Nottingham Playhouse, view of the modern building.

Above: Nottingham Playhouse signage.

Left: Nottingham Playhouse, the older building and tower.

key to the theatre's instant and continuing success. It has a conventional stage but a round auditorium offering remarkable flexibility. The building has had further additions and modifications over the decades since opening.

48. Nottingham College, Canal Street

Like many Further Education colleges, Nottingham College has its origins, in terms of the earlier establishments and merged partner college, back in the early and mid-1900s. Following recent mergers, it became one of the largest FE providers in the UK and also delivers university-level courses too. It presently runs ten Nottingham-based centres around the city, having sold off some sites to fund the building of the 'City Hub' (pictured) on a disused brownfield site by the Broadmarsh Centre and tram overpass at the foot of Lace Market Cliff. This six-storey building was designed by the Sheffield architects, Bond Bryan, and built by Wates of Leatherhead. Institutions such as the college have had many issues and problems in recent years, but they and the universities are at the heart of an emerging international city.

Nottingham College, Canal Street entrance.

Nottingham College main building.

49. East Midlands Conference Centre, Loverose Way

Conferencing is now increasingly important for universities and furthermore, suitable venues are vital to a modern city economy. Established in 1994, the East Midlands Conference Centre is a cornerstone for national and international events, and with a reputation for its architectural elegance with rooms and it has a good variety of rooms with state-of-the-art facilities. Designed within the University of Nottingham main campus it is located adjacent to the Orchard Hotel & Restaurant, the buildings have been upgraded in recent years to a thoroughly modern facility.

Left: East Midlands Conference Centre, University of Nottingham.

Below: East Midlands Conference Centre and Orchard Hotel, University of Nottingham.

East Midlands Conference Centre signage.

50. Jubilee Campus, University of Nottingham, Triumph Road

As noted earlier, the emergence of major universities becomes critical to a city's status and its future. The Jubilee Campus of the University of Nottingham is a dramatic landmark addition to the city's architecture, and opened in 1999, is on the site of the old Raleigh factory. The design competition for a new extension to the university campus was won by architects Michael Hopkins & Partners.

A strikingly modern building at the University of Nottingham's Jubilee Campus.

Incorporating a green roof at the Jubilee Campus.

The lake at the University of Nottingham's Jubilee Campus.

The teaching buildings line the eastern shore of a new lake, and the faculty buildings are clean, simple, and functional as they employ combinations of standard forms. The three-storey blocks have cladding of red cedar with paired atria and a lakeside colonnade. Along with Canadian cedar cladding the 'sustainable' buildings have part-passive heating and cooling with solar and wind power. Innovations included insulation manufactured from used newspapers and the use of green roofs. The result is a very strikingly pleasant site, and the centrepiece is the Learning Resource Centre situated on an island in the lake and accessible via a causeway. It is all rather pleasant as an urban environment in which to work and to learn, and perhaps a vision of how future urban development should be.

Bibliography

There is a huge amount of literature on the history of Nottingham, of its people, its heritage, and its industries. These are just a few sources:

Harwood, E., *Pevsner Architectural Guides* (Nottingham: Yale University Pres, New Haven & London, 2008)

Iliffe, R. and Baguley, W., *Victorian Nottingham: A Story in Pictures* (Nottingham Historical Film Unit, 1970)

Jenkins, S., *England's Thousand Best Houses* (Allen Lane, London, 2003)

Jennings, G., *Nottingham and South Notts on old postcards: Reflections of a Bygone Age* (Keyworth, 1984)

Kaye, D., *A History of Nottinghamshire* (Phillimore & Co. Ltd., Chichester, 1987)

Mellors, R., *In and About Nottinghamshire. A book for the young men and women of the city and county* (J. & H. Bell, Nottingham, 1908)

Oldfield, G., *Britain in Old Photographs: Nottingham Past & Present* (Sutton Publishing Limited, Stroud, 1999)

Payne, M., *Britain in Old Photographs: Victorian Nottingham* (Alan Sutton Publishing Limited, Stroud, 1992)

Pevsner, N., *The Buildings of England. Nottinghamshire* (Penguin Books, Harmondsworth, Middlesex, 1951)

Richards, C., *Nottingham Through Time* (Amberley, Stroud, 2008)

Rotherham, I. D., *Sherwood Forest and the Dukeries. A Companion to the Land of Robin Hood* (Amberley, Stroud, 2013)

Rotherham, I. D., *Lost Nottingham in Colour* (Amberley Publishing, Stroud, 2015)

Rotherham, I. D. and Handley, C., *Historic England: Nottingham* (Amberley Publishing, Stroud, 2018)

Walker, J. H., *Links with Old Nottingham – Historical Notes* (Nottingham Evening News, Nottingham, 1928)

Walker, J., 'The Alan Sillitoe Interview', *LeftLion Magazine* (Nottingham, 2008)
Weir, C., *The Nottinghamshire Heritage* (Phillimore & Co. Ltd, Chichester, 1991)

Websites

britishlistedbuildings.co.uk
historicengland.org.uk
nottingham21.co.uk/Buildings_index.htm
nottinghampost.com
visit-nottinghamshire.co.uk

Acknowledgements

The help and patience of the team at Amberley is much appreciated.

About the Author

Ian Rotherham is Emeritus Professor at the Advanced Wellbeing Research Centre, Sheffield Hallam University. He is an environmental historian and a worldwide authority on ecology, landscape history, tourism, and leisure. Born in Sheffield, Ian established and directed Sheffield City Council's Ecology Service within the City Museums Department, writes for the *Sheffield Star*, *Sheffield Telegraph*, and the *Yorkshire Post* newspapers, and has regular phone-ins on BBC Radio Sheffield and works with the popular media regionally and nationally. Ian has written, edited, and published over a thousand academic papers, articles, books, and book chapters. He lectures widely to local groups and works closely with conservation organisations, agencies, and local authorities. His recent books include *Lost Nottingham in Colour*, *Historic England: Nottingham*, *Sherwood Forest and the Dukeries: A Companion to the Land of Robin Hood*, *Lost Sheffield in Colour*, *The Historic & Heritage Trees of Sherwood Forest in Myth & Legend, in Life & Death*, *Lost York in Colour*, *Secret Sheffield*, *Sheffield Pubs*, and several others for Amberley Publishing.